THE
KITCHEN PANTRY
SCIENTIST

PHYSICS
FOR KIDS

Science **EXPERIMENTS AND ACTIVITIES** Inspired
by **AWESOME PHYSICISTS**, Past and Present

LIZ LEE HEINECKE

QUARRY

Brimming with creative inspiration, how-to projects, and useful information to enrich your everyday life, Quarto Knows is a favorite destination for those pursuing their interests and passions. Visit our site and dig deeper with our books into your area of interest: Quarto Creates, Quarto Cooks, Quarto Homes, Quarto Lives, Quarto Drives, Quarto Explores, Quarto Gifts, or Quarto Kids.

© 2022 Quarto Publishing Group USA Inc.
Text © 2022 Liz Lee Heinecke
Photography © 2022 Quarto Publishing Group USA Inc.

First Published in 2022 by Quarry Books, an imprint of The Quarto Group, 100 Cummings Center, Suite 265-D, Beverly, MA 01915, USA.
T (978) 282-9590 F (978) 283-2742 QuartoKnows.com

Quarry Books titles are also available at discount for retail, wholesale, promotional, and bulk purchase. For details, contact the Special Sales Manager by email at specialsales@quarto.com or by mail at The Quarto Group, Attn: Special Sales Manager, 100 Cummings Center, Suite 265-D, Beverly, MA 01915, USA.

10 9 8 7 6 5 4 3 2 1

ISBN: 978-0-7603-7243-2

Digital edition published in 2022
eISBN: 978-0-7603-7244-9

Library of Congress Cataloging-in-Publication Available

Design: Debbie Berne
Cover Illustrations: Kelly Anne Dalton
Cover Photos: Amber Procaccini Photography
Illustration of author: Mattie Wells (cover and page 3)
Photography: Amber Procaccini Photography
Illustration: Kelly Anne Dalton

Printed in China

PHYSICS
FOR KIDS

*For my dad Ron Lee, the physicist who taught me to love science
and has always encouraged my curiosity about the natural world.*

CONTENTS

INTRODUCTION

Did you ever stop to think about the fact that the force that controls the movement of the planets—gravity—can be overcome by static electricity? Test it for yourself. Run a plastic comb through your hair on a dry day, and then use the comb to attract and lift a tiny piece of paper. Gravity will try to pull the paper back to Earth, but it will be defeated by electricity, which is a much stronger force.

The pull and push of forces, such as gravity and electricity, control our day-to-day universe. The force between electrical charges even controls the chemical properties of atoms, which are the building blocks of everything on Earth. Nuclear forces holding the centers of atoms together are even stronger than the electrostatic force.

Physics is a modern discipline of science that concerns itself with these forces, along with time and space, to describe how our universe, and everything in it, works. *Physics for Kids* will introduce you to twenty-five scientists, from past to present, along with experiments and projects related to their work in physics.

What Pierre Curie learned about piezoelectricity can be tested by crushing a mint to create a flash of light. Squeezing a foam ball will help you understand how stars collapse, and you'll learn how Jocelyn Bell Burnell discovered first pulsar. You can even make a magical illusion transmitter similar to one invented by Valerie L. Thomas by using a concave mirror and glow sticks.

Once you've learned a little bit about the history of physics, you will appreciate how fast our understanding of the universe has advanced over the last few centuries. Since the beginning of time, people have paid attention to the movement of the sun, the moon, the tides, and the changing seasons. Ancient Chinese and Roman people used hourglasses, water clocks, and sundials to measure time. Between 2600 BCE and 300 CE, ancient Egyptians and Nubians used advanced engineering techniques to move enormous granite and sandstone blocks to build spectacular pyramids on the African continent. The Greek philosopher Democritus, born around 460 BCE, came up with the idea of the atom, whose very name means "indivisible," as the smallest building block of space and matter.

Science took flight into the practical world of technology when experiments involving heat, magnets, optics (such as prisms and lenses), and chemistry became popular in the 1500s and 1600s. Famous natural philosophers, such as Galileo, Descartes, and Newton, took measurements and used logic and mathematics to explain what they observed. Then, in the 1700s, mathematics became a common language used to describe the results of experiments.

Physics became its own branch of science, separate from chemistry and "natural philosophy" in the 1800s. Scientists exploring heat, light, magnetism, sound, and electricity discovered that these things had something in common: energy. When modern physics emerged around 1900, time, atoms, X-rays, and radioactivity had become areas of great interest. Today, time can be measured to a thousandth of a trillionth of a second and drives modern technology such as high-speed communication and global positioning systems (GPS).

It's fascinating to imagine what will happen over the next hundred years in physics. Perhaps you will be the one to make the next great discovery. Until then, stay curious and take the advice of physicist Nadya Mason, who said in her 2010 TED talk, "Hands-on thinking connects our understanding, and even our vitality, to the physical world and the things that we use."

Let's do some science!

William Gilbert b. 1544

ELECTRICITY

A LARGE FAMILY

William Gilbert grew up in Colchester, England. He had three siblings, but his mother died when he was young. When his father remarried, his stepmother had seven more children. Fortunate to have been born to a wealthy family, William went off to Cambridge at the age of fourteen to study medicine and natural philosophy.

ROYAL DOCTOR

William graduated as a medical doctor in 1569, and he worked as a physician for most of his life. He traveled to Italy and was interested in tropical medicine, which allowed him to meet many sailors, including the famous explorer Sir Francis Drake. In England, he was the personal physician of Queen Elizabeth the First for the last three years of her life and demonstrated many science experiments for her and the royal court.

"LITTLE EARTHS"

Throughout his life, William was fascinated by scientific theory and used much of his time and money answering questions about natural phenomena. His friendship with sailors, who used magnetic compasses to navigate, led him to ask why the magnetized needles always pointed north. He built spheres from magnetic material called magnetite to explore the question and discovered that compass needles always pointed to one end of his "Little Earths." From this, he correctly hypothesized that the planet Earth is an enormous magnet with two magnetic poles.

ELECTRICITAS

Besides magnetism, William Gilbert studied physical forces, which he was the first to call "electricitas." Experimenting with static electricity, William invented a device, which he named a versorium, that could detect the presence of electrical charge. (See Lab 9.) The device allowed him to observe how heat and humidity affected electricity. He could then test how the same variables affected magnetism.

SOLAR REVOLUTION

In 1543, the year before William Gilbert was born, a scientist named Nicolaus Copernicus published a revolutionary book stating that Earth and the other planets orbit the sun. Until that point, most people believed that the Earth was the center of the universe and that all celestial bodies were spinning around us. They also believed that the stars were somehow glued on to an invisible dome in the heavens.

MAPPING THE MOON

A curious man, Gilbert attempted to map the markings he saw on the surface of the moon. He believed that the light spots were water and the dark spots were land. He also studied the stars, concluding that they are at different distances from Earth and not attached to an invisible dome. He died in the year 1603 in London, probably of a disease called bubonic plague, which killed 30,000 people in London that year.

IN TODAY'S WORLD

Magnets can be found everywhere you look in today's technology. In addition to being essential components in generators and motors, they are used to store data in some computers and help convert electronic signals into sound in speakers. Magnets are also essential in medical diagnosis such as MRI (magnetic resonance imaging).

STATIC ELECTRICITY DETECTOR

Build a versorium similar to the one William Gilbert invented and use it to detect static electricity.

MATERIALS

- Aluminum foil
- Paper cup
- Pencil
- Balloon or a plastic comb

SAFETY TIPS AND HINTS

If you have a latex allergy, use a plastic comb instead of a balloon.

PROTOCOL

1 Cut a piece of aluminum foil 3 inches (8 cm) long and 1 inch (2.5 cm) wide. *Fig. 1.*

2 Fold the foil in half the long way, leaving the open edge loose so a pencil can be inserted. *Fig. 2.*

3 Turn a paper cup upside down and poke a pencil up through the bottom so the lead comes up through the exact center. *Fig. 3.*

4 Place the cup upside down on a flat surface with the lead tip of the pencil sticking out vertically.

5 Balance the folded foil on the lead. When it is level, poke the lead through the foil a tiny bit, so the foil can spin like a clock dial. *Fig. 4.*

6 Rub a balloon on your hair or run a plastic comb through your hair.

7 Hold the balloon or comb 2 to 4 inches (5 to 10 cm) away from the aluminum dial on the versorium to detect static electricity. *Fig. 5 and Fig. 6.*

Fig. 5. Hold an electrically charged balloon near the foil.

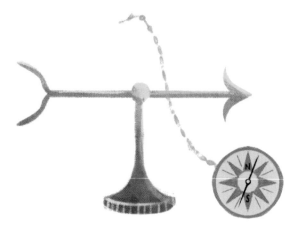

Fig. 1. Cut a long, narrow piece of aluminum foil.

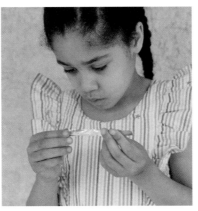

Fig. 2. Fold the foil in half.

Fig. 3. Poke a pencil through the bottom of a cup.

Fig. 4. Balance the folded foil on the pencil lead.

Fig. 6. Watch the foil dial move as it is attracted to or repelled by a charged object.

CREATIVE ENRICHMENT

Build a foil leaf electroscope: Poke a metal nail through some cardboard. Carefully tape on two thin strips of aluminum foil (around 2 inches [5 cm] long and 1 inch [2.5 cm] wide) so they hang down from the nail, just touching each other. Put the cardboard on top of a glass jar so the nail is visible inside the jar and bring a charged object, such as a balloon, close to the head of the nail. Electrons will move through the nail to the foil, giving both strips a similar charge, which will cause them to repel each other and move apart. See below.

THE PHYSICS BEHIND THE FUN

When you comb your hair or rub a balloon on your head, charged particles tinier than atoms jump from strands of hair to the plastic or latex material, creating a buildup of positive or negative charge. This charge is called static electricity and is the same type of charge that can build up on a doorknob to give you a shock.

Objects with opposite charges are attracted to one another. Objects with the same charge push each other away. Negatively charged particles—called electrons—move freely in aluminum. This means when a charged object is placed next to aluminum foil, the charged particles in the foil separate and move to opposite sides of the foil strip. The opposite charges between the balloon and the foil are strong enough to pull the aluminum foil toward the balloon.

Galileo Galilei b. 1564

PENDULUMS

A MUSICIAN

Galileo Galilei was born in 1564 in Pisa, Italy, a city famous for a tall bell tower that leans to one side. His father was a professional musician who played a guitar-like instrument called a lute and composed songs. Galileo learned to play the lute from his father and was exceptionally good at it. Learning musical rhythms was where he first encountered mathematics.

THE SWINGING CHANDELIER

When he was sixteen years old, Galileo went to medical school. His love of numbers distracted him from biology classes and he studied math instead. One day at the cathedral in Pisa, he watched a light fixture swing back and forth on a chain and used his heartbeat to time the swings. As air currents pushed the chandelier new directions, Galileo noticed that small swings took the exact same amount of time as larger ones. It was his first great discovery. Later, Galileo did pivotal experiments with weights hung from fixed points—called pendulums—and came up with rules describing their motion.

FREE FALLING

Fascinated by the physical world, Galileo measured the motion of falling objects. By dropping two spheres with different masses from the tower of Pisa, Galileo famously demonstrated that similar objects fall at the same rate, regardless of mass. He also experimented by rolling balls down ramps. His results later influenced Sir Isaac Newton (Lab 3) as he formulated his well-known laws of motion.

THERMOMETERS AND MOON CRATERS

In addition to experimenting with physics, Galileo was an inventor. He invented an early thermometer, called a thermoscope, created new compasses and balances, and improved the design of telescopes and microscopes. Using telescopes that he modified to increase their magnification,
Galileo was the first person to clearly see craters and mountains on the moon's surface. He was also the first person to record Saturn's rings and Jupiter's moons. Galileo wrote a book about his observations titled *The Starry Messenger.*

THE SUN AS THE CENTER

Galileo's books and ideas made him famous, but they also got him arrested. His research validated a model developed by the astronomer Nicolaus Copernicus in 1543 that put the sun at the center of the universe, with Earth and the other planets revolving around it. This model challenged the Catholic Church's belief that the stars and planets revolved around Earth.

The politically powerful church banned Galileo's books, had him arrested, and gave him a choice: deny his scientific theories or face torture and punishment. Galileo denied his theories, but he continued to write about science in private. Forced to spend the rest of his life under house arrest, he was cared for by one of his daughters until he died at the age of seventy-seven.

IN TODAY'S WORLD

Today, Galileo is considered one of the founders of modern experimental science. In 1996, more than 350 years after his death, the Catholic Church finally admitted that Galileo's ideas about the solar system were correct and that it had made an error in persecuting him.

PLAY WITH PENDULUMS

Test how variables, such as the length of a pendulum or the weight on the end, affect how quickly a pendulum swings back and forth.

MATERIALS

- String, yarn, or twine
- Paper clip
- Tape
- Pencil
- Yard stick or meter stick
- Metal washers or nuts (different sizes, if you have them)
- Timer, such as a phone timer
- Graph paper (optional)

PROTOCOL

1 Cut a piece of string 24 inches (61 cm) long.

2 Tie the paper clip to one end the string, forming it into a hook. *Fig. 1.*

3 Firmly tape the pencil to the edge of a table, so one end is sticking out.

4 Tie the string to the pencil. The point where the string meets the pencil is called the pivot point. *Fig. 2.*

5 Add a metal washer or nut to the hook. On a pendulum, the weight at the end of the string or rod is called the bob. Make sure that the weight can swing freely, parallel to the table.

6 Tape a yard stick or meter stick to the table next to the pendulum, so you can measure how high you pull the weight.

Fig. 5. Count how many times the washer swings back and forth in 30 seconds.

7 Set a timer for 30 seconds.

Pull the washer up and out so the string is tight and at an angle of about 45 degrees from the tabletop. Use the yard stick to measure how far from the floor you pull the weight, so you can repeat the experiment. *Fig. 3.*

8 Let go of the weight as you start the timer and count how many times the washer swings back and forth in 30 seconds. Record the number of swings. *Fig. 4 and Fig. 5.*

9 Multiply by 2 to calculate swings per minute. This number is called the period of the pendulum.

10 Add a second weight to the hook and repeat the experiment by pulling the weight to the same height to test whether doubling the weight changes the number of swings per minute. Remember to multiply your count by 2.

11 Compare the two measurements. Did adding weight change the period (number of swings per minute) of the pendulum?

Fig. 1. Tie a paper clip to one end of a string.

Fig. 2. Tie the string to a pencil taped onto a table.

Fig. 3. Add a metal washer or nut to the hook and pull it out to a 45-degree angle.

Fig. 4. Start the timer as you release the weight.

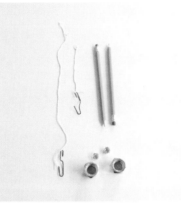

Fig. 6. Cut a second string, half the length, and repeat the experiment.

CREATIVE ENRICHMENT

Test several pendulum lengths. Graph your results with pendulum length on one axis and swings per minute (period) on the other axis.

12 Cut a second string, half the length (12 inches [30 cm] long) of the first one. Repeat the experiment to measure the effect of a shorter distance between the pencil (the pivot) and the bob (the weight). *Fig. 6.*

13 Compare the period of the shorter pendulum with that of the longer pendulum. What did you find?

THE PHYSICS BEHIND THE FUN

A pendulum is a hanging object on a string or chain attached to a fixed point called a pivot. A pendulum could be a hanging light fixture or a playground swing. The amount of time it takes for the object to swing from its starting point back to its original position is called the period of the pendulum.

Gravity is the main force acting on the pendulum. When an object hangs straight down on a pendulum, it is at rest, or equilibrium. If you pull it up, gravity wants to pull it back down, and it will swing back and forth until it is once again at rest.

A pendulum's period depends on the length of the string, but not on the mass (weight) of the swinging object. Adding weight to the string does not change the period of the pendulum. Changing the length of the string, however, will shorten or lengthen the period.

SIMPLE THERMOMETER

Use an empty bottle, a drinking straw, and a water–alcohol mixture to assemble a home-made thermometer.

MATERIALS

- Masking tape or a label
- Permanent marker
- Clear, empty bottle
- Clear drinking straw
- Ruler
- Water
- Rubbing alcohol (isopropanol)
- Red food coloring
- Playdough or sculpting clay

SAFETY TIPS AND HINTS

- Do this project in a well-ventilated area.
- Adult supervision is required when using rubbing alcohol to make a thermometer. Rubbing alcohol is dangerous if ingested. Dump the alcohol and water mixture down the sink when you have finished the project.

Fig. 7. Place the thermascope in ice water and then in warm water to observe how the column level changes.

PROTOCOL

1 Label an empty bottle "Warning: Contains rubbing alcohol."

2 Use a permanent marker to make marks ½ inch (1 cm) apart on the straw. *Fig. 1.*

3 Mix ¼ cup (60 ml) of water with ¼ cup (60 ml) of rubbing alcohol in the empty bottle. Add several drops of red food coloring. Put the straw in the bottle. *Fig. 2 and Fig. 3.*

4 Use playdough to seal the mouth of the bottle, keeping the straw suspended ¼ inch (6 mm) above the bottom of the bottle. Wrap a little bit of clay around the top of the straw, leaving the hole open. *Fig. 4 and Fig. 5.*

5 Pour a little bit of water into the straw so that it is about halfway to the top. If your seal is tight, the water will form a column in the straw and the level will remain stable. Allow the water to mix with the alcohol solution. Label the liquid level as room temperature. *Fig. 6.*

6 Place the thermometer in a bowl of ice water for 2 minutes and observe the level of the red liquid in the straw. *Fig. 7.*

7 Move the thermometer to a bowl of warm water and check the level.

8 Finally, put the thermoscope in a bowl of hot tap water to see how the level of the red fluid changes.

Fig. 1. Mark a straw with lines ½ inch (1 cm) apart.

Fig. 2. Mix water and rubbing alcohol in an empty bottle labeled with a warning.

Fig. 3. Add several drops of food coloring.

Fig. 4. Seal the mouth of the bottle, keeping the straw suspended.

Fig. 5. For safety, put more clay around the tip of the straw, but keep the opening clear.

Fig. 6. Add a little water to the straw to form a column. Mark level as room temperature.

CREATIVE ENRICHMENT

Using a real thermometer as a reference, add more temperature markings to your homemade thermometer.

THE PHYSICS BEHIND THE FUN

If you take apart the word thermometer, *thermo* means "heat" and *meter* comes from the Latin word *metrum*, which means "to measure." The thermoscope originally built by Galileo was made of a glass bulb with a hollow stem that sat in a vase filled with water. When the air in the bulb warmed up, the air pressure inside got higher and pushed water out of the stem, into the bulb, so less water in the stem indicated a hotter temperature.

In this lab, red alcohol is sealed inside a container to create a simple thermometer. Liquids take up less space when they are cold and take up more space when they are warm. When the temperature inside the bottle increases, air pressure increases and the liquid expands, pushing alcohol up the straw. Alcohol works better than water in thermometers because it will not freeze at low temperatures.

$$m_1 \xrightarrow{\ } \quad \xleftarrow{\ } m_2$$
$$\vec{F_1} \qquad\qquad \vec{F_2}$$
$$\longleftarrow \quad r \quad \longrightarrow$$
$$F_1 = F_2 = G \, \frac{m_1 \times m_2}{r^2}$$

Sir Isaac Newton b. 1643

GRAVITY AND PRISMS

A SMALL BOY

Isaac Newton was born in a small village in Lincolnshire, England, in 1643. A small child who was born prematurely, he would grow up to be a giant of science and mathematics. Isaac's father died three months before he was born, and he did not get along his stepfather. Luckily, building things such as grinding mills powered by mice running on wheels entertained him and distracted him from his problems. Isaac was bullied in school, but it only made him work harder.

A PLAGUE

After trying his hand at farming, which he did not enjoy, Isaac went to college at Trinity College, Cambridge, in 1661. An average student, Isaac learned about the work of Galileo (Lab 2) and Johannes Kepler, who described the orbits of the planets around the sun. His education was interrupted in 1665, when a deadly disease called bubonic plague broke out in London and spread through the city. The threat of plague, which was spread by fleas infected with *Yersinia pestis* bacteria, caused Trinity College to close for almost two years, and Isaac returned home to the countryside.

AN APPLE

Isaac's two years at home proved to be the most important time of his life. Besides playing with mathematical concepts and experimenting with light, he had an extraordinary thought one day while sitting in the garden. Why, he wondered, do apples always fall straight down from the tree, as if being drawn to the center of the Earth? He questioned whether the force pulling a falling apple to the ground was strong enough to pull on distant objects, such as the moon. This idea would be central to a theory he later described using math; it's called the law of universal gravitation.

A RAINBOW

Newton's experiments with light demonstrated for the first time that white light is made up of every color of light in the rainbow. He demonstrated this by poking a hole in a curtain and holding a piece of cut glass called a prism in front of the sunlight streaming through the hole. The result was a beautiful rainbow of light, each color separated by the glass. The experiment made him realize that glass telescope lenses made images blurry by separating the colors out, and he invented a telescope made using mirrors that gave much sharper images of distant objects.

PRINCIPIA

Isaac Newton became a professor of mathematics at Cambridge. Using math, including a type of math he had invented, called calculus, Isaac described the way objects moved and the effect of gravity on distant objects, such as the moon. In 1687, he wrote a famous book called *Mathematical Principles of Natural Philosophy*, or *Principia Mathematica*, which included many of his most famous ideas, including his law of universal gravitation, the motion of the planets, and his three laws of motion describing inertia, acceleration, and action/reaction. Sir Isaac Newton died in 1727, when he was eighty-four years old. Although he was a small boy from a small town, he had created the foundation of modern mathematics and physics.

IN TODAY'S WORLD

The Hubble Telescope, orbiting high above Earth, is a reflecting telescope. A highly evolved model of the one first invented by Sir Isaac Newton, the powerful telescope uses curved mirrors to detect and focus light. The Hubble has been sending images from distant galaxies to scientists around the world since 1990.

CENTER OF GRAVITY

Use two intertwined forks to create an amazing balancing trick using a toothpick on the edge of a glass.

MATERIALS

- 2 metal forks
- Several toothpicks
- Wine glass or curved glass
- Lighter or match

SAFETY TIPS AND HINTS

Adult supervision is required for the fork-balancing enrichment activity. Long hair should be pulled back.

PROTOCOL

1 Push the tines of two forks together tightly, so the tines are curving outward. It will take some work to get the hang of it. *Fig. 1.*

2 Insert a toothpick through the top two tines of the forks. *Fig. 2.*

3 Balance the toothpick and forks on one finger first. This may take a few tries. *Fig. 3.*

4 Now balance the toothpick and forks of the edge of a wine glass or curved glass. *Fig. 4.*

5 The center of gravity is in the space between the forks and the glass. *Fig. 5.*

Fig. 4. Balance the toothpick and forks on the edge of a curved glass.

THE PHYSICS BEHIND THE FUN

Every object on Earth, whether it is a boat, a person on a bike, or two forks attached to a toothpick, has a single point called the center of gravity (or center of mass), which gravity acts on. This fun trick demonstrates how you can balance the mass, of two forks and a toothpick sitting on the edge of a wineglass.

The center of gravity on a curved glass exists in the space between the glass and the forks. If you light the toothpick inside the glass on fire, it will burn out when the flame hits the cooling glass. Because the toothpick is so light—has very little mass—the center of gravity doesn't change much, so the forks remain balanced.

Fig. 1. Intertwine the tines of two forks.

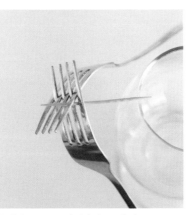

Fig. 2. Insert a toothpick through the top two tines.

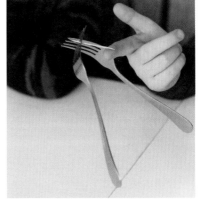

Fig. 3. Balance the toothpick and forks on a finger.

Fig. 5. The center of gravity is in the space between the forks and the glass.

CREATIVE ENRICHMENT

With adult supervision and long hair pulled back, light the toothpick inside the glass by using a lighter or match. It will burn to the edge of the glass and go out, but the forks will remain balanced on the glass. *Fig. 6 and Fig. 7.*

Fig. 6. With adult supervision, light the toothpick inside the glass on fire.

Fig. 7. The forks will remain balanced.

PRISM RAINBOWS

Use transparent objects called prisms to separate light waves into a spectrum of beautiful colors.

MATERIALS

- Piece of black or white paper
- 2 triangular prisms (Inexpensive glass prisms can be purchased online.)
- 2 boxes, such as cereal boxes

SAFETY TIPS AND HINTS

Photograph the beautiful light waves you produce using the prisms. This project works best in the morning or evening when the sunlight is at a low angle.

PROTOCOL

1 Find an area where there is bright sunlight. Set a piece of black paper in the light. *Fig. 1.*

2 Put one prism on the black paper with the triangular edges facing up and down.

3 Turn the prism until you find an angle that separates the light waves into a rainbow. *Fig. 2.*

4 Place the second prism in the rainbow to see what happens. *Fig. 3.*

5 Arrange two boxes so there is a narrow beam of light coming from between them.

6 Set one prism in the beam of light and use the second prism to create rainbows and colors. *Fig. 4 and Fig. 5.*

7 Play with the angles of the prisms. Try to produce beams of a single color. *Fig. 6 and Fig. 7.*

Fig. 7. Try to separate beams of individual colors.

Fig. 1. Place a prism on black paper in the sunlight.

Fig. 2. Find an angle that separates light waves into a rainbow of colors.

Fig. 3. Put a second prism in the rainbow you made.

Fig. 4. Use the prisms to play with light waves.

Fig. 5. Describe the colors you see.

Fig. 6. Observe how changing the angle of the prisms changes the light patterns.

THE PHYSICS BEHIND THE FUN

Sir Isaac Newton was the first to demonstrate that white light contains all the colors of the rainbow. He visualized light as a particle, but he was only partly right. Later experiments with light (Lab 6) demonstrated that light travels through space as a wave. You can think of light moving like waves on a lake. Each color in a rainbow has a certain wavelength, or distance between light waves.

The word *refraction* describes the bending of light as it moves from air through different mediums, such as glass. The bending occurs because different colors of light (wavelengths) travel through glass at different speeds. How much the light speed changes depends on wavelength. The shortest wavelength visible to humans is violet, and those light waves bend the most. Red light waves are the longest and bend the least. The other colors fall between violet and red.

When sunlight, which normally appears white, travels through a prism, the light waves bend and are dispersed, or spread out, by the prism to create a rainbow of color with violet on one end and red on the other. A second prism can be used to reflect and bend the light waves to separate out individual colors.

Laura Bassi b. 1711

AIR AND ELECTRICITY

A DEBATE

Europe's first female university professor, Laura Bassi, was born to a middle-class family in Bologna, Italy, in 1711. She was the only surviving child in her family, and although she never attended school, she was tutored in math, languages, literature, and natural philosophy from the time she was five years old. Although girls were not treated equally at that time, people recognized that she had an extraordinary mind and Laura was invited to publicly debate four professors from the University of Bologna when she was only nineteen years old.

MINERVA

At twenty, Laura became the first woman to receive a doctoral degree in science from the University of Bologna, and was made a professor at the same time. She was a celebrity. Several paintings commemorated the occasion, along with a bronze medal featuring Laura's face. People called her Minerva of Bologna, after the Roman goddess of wisdom and learning, and scholars and other travelers came from far and wide to meet her.

A LABORATORY

Although she was a professor and a member of the Italian Institute of Science, Laura was not allowed to lecture in public without the permission of men at the university. Because society would allow her more freedom to converse with other scholars as a married woman, she agreed to marry the physician Giuseppe Veratti. He had promised via letter that he would not "hinder her in her studies." She set up a laboratory in their house, where she taught and did experiments. Laura Bassi had eight children, but there were no vaccines against childhood diseases and three of them died.

AIR AND ELECTRICITY

As an experimental physicist, Laura Bassi was fascinated by the discoveries of Sir Isaac Newton (Lab 3). She was especially intrigued by his work with light and sometimes did public demonstrations of his experiments. Because she was interested in the relationship between light, air, and electricity, some of her own experiments involved studying bubbles that formed in liquids, and whether they were attracted to the walls of containers due to electrical forces.

A FORCE

Laura and Giuseppe had an "electrical machine" in their laboratory that made it possible for them to do groundbreaking research at home. They conducted dangerous experiments on atmospheric electricity at their country house, after experiments with lightning were banned in the city of Bologna. Laura authored at least twenty-eight papers in her career. Most involved Newtonian mechanics, but seven of her papers were focused on electricity. She exchanged letters with Alessandro Volta, who created the first battery. Volta was a great admirer of her work.

A CHAIR

When Laura Bassi was sixty-five, she was finally named the chair of physics at the University of Bologna. She died two years later at the age of sixty-seven.

IN TODAY'S WORLD

Static electricity is used in some factories to remove pollutants from smokestacks and pipes. Tiny particles can be charged and then exposed to a metal collection plate containing the opposite charge, which pulls them out of the air before it enters the atmosphere.

BOIL WATER AT ROOM TEMPERATURE

Use a syringe and your finger to create a vacuum that causes bubbles to form at room temperature.

MATERIALS

- Small glass
- Plastic syringe (Large syringes work best and can be purchased at pharmacies or online.)
- Tap water, chilled and room temperature
- Carbonated water, chilled and room temperature
- Soda pop, chilled and room temperature

PROTOCOL

1 Fill a small glass with water.

2 Pull water into the syringe until it is around two-thirds of the way full. *Fig. 1.*

3 Tip the syringe up, and then push or flick air bubbles out. *Fig. 2.*

4 Place a finger over the end of the syringe. With your other hand, slowly pull down on the syringe plunger to create a vacuum. Observe the bubbles that form in the liquid. *Fig. 3.*

5 Keeping your finger over the end, release the plunger to allow it to return to its original position. See what happens to the bubbles.

6 Pull the syringe back a second time. Do the bubbles form more quickly?

7 Repeat the experiment with carbonated water and then with soda. Compare how bubbles form, dissolve, or remain in the liquid. *Fig. 4 and Fig. 5.*

8 Test how temperature affects bubble formation and redissolving by repeating the experiment using very cold liquids versus warm ones.

Fig. 6. Study bubble formation in different containers.

CREATIVE ENRICHMENT

Laura Bassi was curious about why bubbles in liquids formed on different surfaces. Replicate her historical experiment by adding carbonated water or soda pop to clear containers with different shapes. How do bubbles form in a champagne glass versus a wine glass? A rectangular vase versus one with a narrow neck? Note: Champagne glasses are made with tiny scratches at the bottom that allow for bubble to form easily. *Fig. 6.*

Fig. 1. Pull water into a syringe.

Fig. 2. Push and flick air bubbles out.

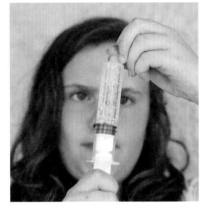

Fig. 3. Plug the syringe and pull down on the plunger.

Fig. 4. Repeat the experiment with carbonated liquid.

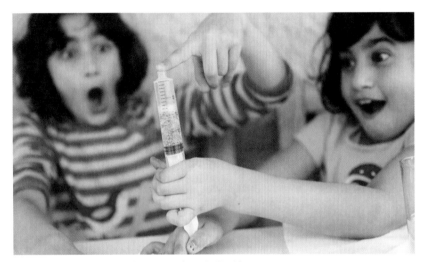

Fig. 5. Observe the bubbles that emerge from the liquid.

THE PHYSICS BEHIND THE FUN

Boiling is defined as the phase transition from the liquid state to the gas state. In this experiment, you are boiling water at room temperature by decreasing the pressure on liquid in a syringe.

Tap water, carbonated water, and soda all contain dissolved gases. Tap water contains mostly the gases found in air, which consists of around 78% nitrogen, 21% oxygen, and a few other gases. Carbonated water and soda pop are fizzy because they contain carbon dioxide gas. Colder water allows more gas to dissolve inside it. When liquid water boils, gas bubbles that contain water vapor form. Water vapor is the gaseous form of water.

Putting a finger over the syringe and pulling on the plunger increases the space (volume) inside the syringe and lowers the pressure inside, forming a partial vacuum that contains only water vapor. Gases dissolved inside the liquid escape from the liquid to form bubbles. When the plunger is released, the pressure inside the syringe increases again. Some of the gas will remain in the syringe as large bubbles, but tiny bubbles containing lots of water vapor redissolve into the liquid.

DANCING BUBBLES AND STATIC ELECTRICITY

Blow bubbles on a smooth surface and use an electrically charged balloon to make them move.

MATERIALS

- Balloon
- Drinking straw
- Bubble solution

PROTOCOL

1 Blow up a balloon.

2 Dip the end of the straw in bubble mixture.

3 Put your mouth on the other end of the straw and gently blow a big bubble on a smooth plate or tray. *Fig. 1 and Fig. 2.*

4 Rub the balloon on your hair to give it an electrical charge. *Fig. 3.*

5 Hold the balloon near the bubble to see whether you can make it move without touching it. If it pops, try again! *Fig. 4, and Fig. 5.*

6 Test the charged balloon by using different-size bubbles to see what happens.

Fig. 1. Use a straw to blow a bubble on a flat, smooth surface.

THE PHYSICS BEHIND THE FUN

Rubbing a balloon on your hair causes charged particles called electrons to jump between your hair and the balloon, leaving an electrical charge on the balloon. Bubbles are made of a liquid shell. When you put a charged balloon next to a bubble, charged particles move around in the bubble so that the side of the bubble closest to the balloon has an opposite charge and is attracted to the balloon. This attractive charge pulls the bubble toward the balloon.

Fig. 2. Blow a bubble on a plate.

Fig. 3. Rub a balloon on your hair to give it an electrical charge.

Fig. 4. Hold the electrically charged balloon near the bubble to make it move.

Fig. 5. If it pops, try again.

CREATIVE ENRICHMENT

Blow a bubble inside another bubble. Does the static charge on the balloon move both? How many bubbles in bubbles can you make? *Fig. 6.*

Fig. 6. Blow a bubble inside the bubble. How many bubbles can you blow inside a single bubble?

Benjamin Thompson (Count Rumford) b. 1753

THERMODYNAMICS

A VILLAGE SCHOOL

Despite being known as Count Rumford, Benjamin Thompson was not born a count. Benjamin arrived in this world in 1753 in Woburn, Massachusetts, just north of Boston. His father died before he turned two. Although Benjamin went to the village school, his teacher was educated at Harvard University, which was only ten miles away, and Benjamin attended some lectures there.

AN UNCERTAIN FUTURE

Although he was interested in math and science, Benjamin went to work as an apprentice for a businessman who sold dry goods, and then trained with a medical doctor. Unhappy with his work, he moved to Concord, New Hampshire, to establish a school. Within a few months, he married a wealthy woman named Sarah Rolfe. Her money allowed him to stop teaching and become a "gentleman" who was free to spend his time as he pleased.

A SPY FOR THE ENEMY

Near the beginning of the American Revolutionary War, Benjamin was exposed as a Loyalist who sided with the British. When he heard that a mob was coming to tar and feather him, he escaped on his brother-in-law's horse, leaving his wife and daughter behind. Benjamin then went to Boston, where he was a spy and informant for the British army. In 1775, he left for England, where he studied gunpowder, published papers on his findings, and became a respected scientist.

RUMFORD'S SOUP

Following the war, Benjamin moved to Bavaria and turned his talents to helping people, rather than hurting them. To help the poor and homeless, he established free schools for children, started industrial and veterinary schools, and encouraged gardening, rotating crops, and growing potatoes. Benjamin invented a nutritious stew for the poor, which was nicknamed "Rumford's soup." While experimenting with light, heating, and cooking, he invented the drip coffeepot. He also created a beautiful public park in Munich; it still stands today.

A HEATED REVOLUTION

In 1791, Benjamin Thompson was made a count and people called him "Count Rumford." He disagreed with a popular idea that heat was a liquid which could neither be created or destroyed. Instead, Benjamin believed that heat could be created by motion. At that time, cannons were made by boring (drilling) out the center of metal cylinders to make hollow barrels. He bored out a cannon barrel underwater to demonstrate that after two and half hours, enough heat was produced to boil the water holding the cannon barrel. This was the beginning of a revolution in thermodynamics, which is the science of heat.

FIRE AND SHADOW

Count Rumford redesigned fireplaces to make them smaller, less smoky, and more efficient. He also re-engineered industrial furnaces and improve chimney design. Dividing his time between England and France, he studied the measurement of light and what happened when different color shadows were combined. Rumford established the Royal Institution of Great Britain. He died in 1814 and his daughter Sarah became "Countess Rumford."

IN TODAY'S WORLD

Drip coffee pots and sous-vide cooking were both invented by Count Rumford. His inventions continue to make our world warmer and more delicious today.

HEAT DRILLS AND FRICTION

Make a simple heat drill to measure temperature changes caused by friction.

MATERIALS

- Hammer
- Large nail
- Piece of wood or wood block, such a scrap of pine or hardwood
- Wooden dowel or unvarnished (disposable) wooden chopstick
- Ruler (optional)
- Instant-read thermometer with metal tip

SAFETY TIPS AND HINTS

- Test the skewer or chopstick to make sure there are no splinters.
- Small children should be supervised when they are useing a hammer and nails.

Fig. 4. Spin a chopstick or dowel in the nail hole to create friction.

PROTOCOL

1 Use the hammer and nail to make a deep indentation in the wood, around ½ inch (1 cm) deep. *Fig. 1.*

2 With the nail, widen the opening so that the dowl or chopstick end will fit inside.

3 About 2 inches (5 cm) from the nail hole, use the nail and a ruler to scrape a straight groove in the wood, 4 inches (10 cm) long. *Fig. 2.*

4 Use the thermometer to measure the temperature inside the nail hole and the groove. Record the reading. *Fig. 3.*

5 Put the pointed end of the dowel or chopstick in the hole and spin it back and forth rapidly between your palms, as if you were trying to start a fire. *Fig. 4.*

6 After 1 minute, measure the temperature in the nail hole. *Fig. 5.*

7 Place the pointed end of the chopstick or one end of the dowel in the groove you made and slide it back and forth rapidly for 1 minute, pushing down slightly on the chopstick to add pressure.

8 Measure the temperature in the groove by laying the thermometer inside the groove. Compare the temperature in the nail hole to the temperature in the groove. *Fig. 6 and Fig. 7.*

Fig. 1. Use a hammer and nail to make a deep indent in a piece of wood.

Fig. 2. Use a nail and ruler to scrape a deep, straight groove in the wood.

Fig. 3. Measure the temperature in the nail hole and the groove.

Fig. 5. Measure the temperature in the nail hole again.

Fig. 6. Slide the dowel in the groove to create pressure and friction.

Fig. 7. Measure the temperature in the groove.

CREATIVE ENRICHMENT

Look up instructions and make a pressure drill for starting campfires.

THE PHYSICS BEHIND THE FUN

No surface is perfectly smooth. If your rub your hands together quickly, you will feel them getting warmer because of a phenomenon called friction. Friction is the resistance between two objects that are in contact with each other. Rough surfaces create more friction than smooth ones, and when two objects are pushed together with more force, additional friction is created.

As two surfaces such as a wooden dowel and a scrap of wood move against each other, the friction between surfaces transforms kinetic energy (the energy of motion) into thermal (heat) energy. Adding pressure to the equation, whether by adding weight or pushing down, increases the heat produced by motion. Rubbing or spinning two pieces of wood together quickly enough under pressure can create enough heat to start a fire.

= LAB 6 =
Thomas Young b. 1773
WAVE THEORY

AN INHERITANCE

Thomas Young was born in a small cloth-manufacturing village called Milverton in Somerset, England. By the time he was fourteen years old, he had learned the Greek and Latin languages. When Thomas was nineteen, he went to medical school and then studied at Emmanuel College, Cambridge. In 1797, his uncle, who was also a physician, died, leaving him his estate. Thomas no longer had to worry about money and could freely pursue his scientific interests.

INTERFERENCE PATTERNS

Thomas became a professor of natural philosophy at the Royal Institute in London, where he focused his work on physics. He was interested in light, color, and energy, but he also studied the stretchiness, or elasticity, of materials. Thomas was interested in the patterns made by waves crossing each other in a ripple tank, which were called interference patterns. He used his observations to study light, which he believed moved in waves, like water does.

A BOLD CHALLENGE

In 1803, Thomas published a set of experiments demonstrating that light acts as a wave. In an early experiment, Young covered a window with a piece of paper with a tiny hole in it so that a thin beam of light passed through the hole. He held a small card in the light beam to split it in two. Light passing on one side of the card interacted with light from the other side of the card to create colorful patterns, which he called interference fringes, on the opposite wall.

A more complicated experiment showed that sunlight coming through two thin parallel slits created an interference pattern like the one he had observed in water. His results challenged the theory of Sir Isaac Newton's (Lab 3) that light is made up of particles. Thomas went on to show light interference on soap and oil films.

VISIONARY

By putting together what he knew about the human eye and the physics of light and color, Thomas Young became the first person to figure out how people see color. He proposed that the retina of the human eye contains three types of nerve cells. One type of cell detects blue, another detects green, and the third detects red, allowing humans to see all the colors in the visible light spectrum. Thomas also found that the curvature of the lens of the human eye changes to accommodate near and far vision.

PHYSICS, HIEROGLYPHICS, AND MUSIC

In addition to studying light, color, and vision, Thomas Young came up with theories about how fluids behave. A lover of linguistics, he compared the grammar and vocabulary of 400 languages and helped to untangle the mystery of hieroglyphics. He was on the team that deciphered a famous archeological object called the Rosetta Stone. Thomas even developed a new way of tuning instruments, called "Young's Temperament," which made harmonies sound more perfect in certain keys.

"THE MAN WHO KNEW EVERYTHING"

Thomas Young died when he was only fifty-six years old, but his numerous discoveries and theories were hugely influential. His work lived on long after he was gone. Many great thinkers, including Albert Einstein (Lab 11) were influenced by Young, who had been nicknamed "the man who knew everything."

IN TODAY'S WORLD

Thomas Young's multiple contributions to the diverse fields of physics, biology, language, and music were instrumental to the development of our modern understanding of science and human culture.

LIGHT INTERFERENCE

Observe wave patterns in water, and then experiment with fringe patterns created by light waves as they move through slits.

MATERIALS

- Clear, flat container, such as an 8- x 12-inch (20- x 30-cm) or 9- x 9-inch (23- x 23-cm) glass baking dish
- White paper
- Sharp pencil or ballpoint pen
- White index cards
- Pin, such as a safety pin
- 2 boxes, such as cereal boxes
- Sharp blade, such as a utility knife
- Lamp with single-filament clear bulb (optional)
- Black paper (optional)
- Aluminum foil (optional)
- Tape

Fig. 4. Vary the distance from the wall or paper to observe how the image changes.

SAFETY TIPS AND HINTS

This project workes best when the sun is at a low angle (morning or evening).Adult supervision is recommended for using the utility knife.

PROTOCOL

1 Pour 1 to 2 inches (2.5 to 5 cm) of water into a glass dish and set it on a white piece of paper in a sunny spot.

2 With your finger, touch the water in the center of the edge nearest to you. Observe the wave patterns on the water. This represents how light travels after passing through a single slit or pinhole.

3 To see how light waves create interference patterns after passing through two slits or pinholes simultaneously, touch the water with two fingers at the same time. First, try it with your fingers about 3 inches (7.5 cm) apart and then play with the distance to see what happens. *Fig. 1.*

4 To perform an experiment similar to Thomas Young's, use a sharp pencil or ballpoint pen to poke a hole in the center of an index card. The hole should be around ⅛ inch (3 mm) in diameter. Push down rough edges, so the hole is smooth and round.

5 Find a strong sunbeam indoors or outdoors. This project works well in the morning when sunlight is coming through windows and falling on walls and tabletops.

6 Tape a white index card or white piece of paper to a surface in direct sunlight.

7 Hold the punctured card in the sunlight until you find an angle that allows the light to pass through the hole and project a bright spot on the white paper.

8 Hold a second card perpendicular to the first card so it divides the hole in the card in half, splitting the beam of light coming through the hole. (To make this easier, you can tape the second card onto the card with the hole, using tape and paper.) *Fig. 2.*

Adjust the angle so you can see "fringes" of light on either side of the dot in the middle. These fringes are caused by light wave interference.

Fig. 1. Observe wave patterns in water.

Fig. 2. Punch a hole in an index card and tape a second card to the center, dividing the hole.

Fig. 3. Hold the card in the sunlight and play with the angle to see "fringes" on either side of the spot of light coming through the hole.

Fig. 5. The fringes are caused by light wave interference.

Fig. 6. Tape paper to two boxes.

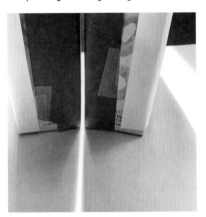

Fig. 7. Use the boxes to collimate light.

Change the distance from the wall or table to see what happens to the image. *Fig. 3 – Fig. 5.*

9 Collimating light directs parallel rays into a narrow beam. Tape paper onto the sides of two boxes and place them in a sunbeam on a table or counter top. Adjust the angle of the boxes to collimate the light so a narrow beam falls on a white surface. *Fig. 6 and Fig. 7.*

10 Repeat steps 7 to 8 using collimated light. You may be able to see colors in the fringes. *Fig. 8.*

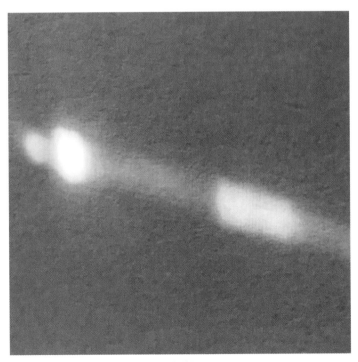

Fig. 8. You may be able to see colors in the fringes.

Fig. 9. Cut two parallel slits in an index card.

Fig. 10. Collimate sunlight onto a white surface, such as paper.

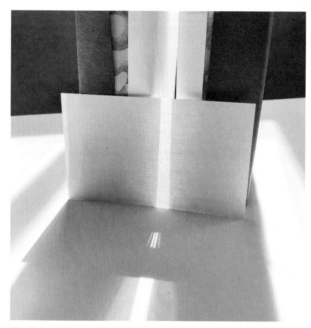

Fig. 11. Study the interference patterns formed by the light.

PART 2

1 Use two boxes to collimate light, as you did in step 9 above.

2 With a sharp blade, cut two parallel slits in an index card, about 1 mm apart and ½ inch (1 cm) long. Use the blade to reinforce the cuts so that when you hold them up to the light, you can see two distinct slits. *Fig. 9.*

3 On a second index card, make two pinholes, as close together as possible.

4 Put a piece of white paper on a flat surface, so that the collimated lights beam falls on the paper. *Fig. 10.*

5 Hold the index cards, one at a time, in the light beam, or set them on a flat surface so you can see the light coming through the slits or dots on the white paper. Play with the distance and angle to create light interference "fringe" patterns on the white paper. *Fig. 11.*

6 Observe a dot of sunlight projected on a wall or tabletop (Part 1 of this Lab) through the double-slit card you created. Or from several feet away, view a clear lightbulb with a single filament by looking through the index cards with double slits or pinholes. Do you see fringes?

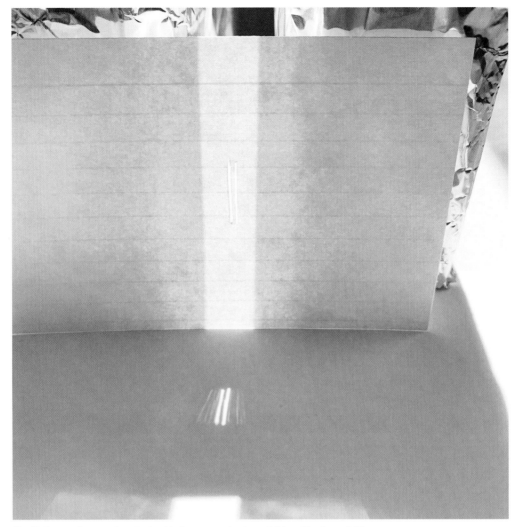

Fig. 12. Repeat the experiment using black paper or aluminum foil to collimate sunlight.

CREATIVE ENRICHMENT

Tape black paper to one side of each box. Repeat Parts 1 and 2 of this lab using light collimated through black paper to see how it changes the images you see. Next, tape aluminum foil to the boxes to observe the effect of light collimated through a reflective surface. *Fig. 12.*

THE PHYSICS BEHIND THE FUN

Today, scientists understand that light behaves as both a particle and a wave. In the first part of this lab, splitting a beam of sunlight coming through a pinhole with an index card creates interference fringes similar to those seen by Thomas Young.

Light waves from the left side of the card interfere with light waves from the right side of the card to create interference fringes containing lines and colors. These patterns are created when certain wavelengths are cancelled out and others are amplified. See Lab 3 to learn more about color and light.

Sending a beam of light through two slits creates more definite interference patterns. If you look through the double slits at a clear lightbulb in a dark room, you will observe interference fringes from the electric light waves.

Augustin-Jean Fresnel b. 1788
LIGHT AND COLOR

A SLOW LEARNER

When Augustin-Jean Fresnel was born in a small village in Normandy, France, no one suspected that he would one day grow up to make great strides in the study of light waves. A sickly child who had contracted the disease tuberculosis at a young age, he was homeschooled along with his three brothers. Augustin was bad at memorization and considered a slow learner, but he enjoyed designing and building things, and he surprised people by constructing sophisticated bows and arrows using tree branches.

BUILDING BRIDGES

At the age of thirteen, Augustin began his formal schooling. Although he struggled with his health, he discovered a talent for drawing and geometry. These skills helped him become a civil engineer who designed and built roads and bridges. As an adult, he worked for the country of France. He felt that his job as an engineer aligned closely with his strong religious belief that one should always work to help others.

AN ENLIGHTENING HOBBY

In 1812, while working to build a highway between Spain and Italy, Fresnel became interested in a new phenomenon he had heard about: the polarization of light. When the Hundred Days War broke out in France, he returned home to live with his mother and did experiments on his own. Many of the papers on polarization were in English, so Augustin could not read them, but he figured out how to study the rainbow of colors produced by focusing sunlight on a drop of honey. He observed colorful shadows, called fringes, produced by the light waves interacting with the golden liquid.

ILLUMINATING SHADOWS

Augustin discovered that when he shined a light on a thin wire, the shadows cast behind the wire contained color. He found that when he held a black piece of paper against one side of the wire, the rainbow shadows disappeared. This suggested that the light had to shine around both sides of the wire to create color and reinforced Thomas Young's (Lab 6) idea that light moved in waves that could interfere with other light waves.

DIFFRACTION

When light waves encounter obstacles or move through another medium, such as glass or water, they bend. Fresnel called this bending diffraction. His experiments, built on the work of Thomas Young, used mathematical equations to describe his observations. The paper he wrote about his work won the grand prize in 1819 at the French Academy of Sciences and inspired the famous mathematician/scientist Siméon Poisson to independently confirm Fresnel's theory that light travels in waves.

A LUMINARY

Augustin Fresnel used what he had learned about bending light to create lenses for lighthouses. These used concentric rings of glass prisms to focus light into an intense beam bright enough to cut through fog and storms. He died of tuberculosis when he was only thirty-nine, just after being awarded the Rumford Medal from the Royal Society of London for his discoveries about the behavior of light.

IN TODAY'S WORLD

Fresnel lighthouse lenses are similar to today's Fresnel lenses, which are found in car taillights, backup lights, and lighting for movies and theaters.

LIGHT WAVE INTERFERENCE

Blow giant bubbles to observe the colors produced by interference of light waves.

MATERIALS

- Clear glass of water
- Pencil
- Around 54 inches (137 cm) of cotton kitchen twine
- 2 dowels or sticks 1–3 feet (30–90 cm) long
- Metal washers
- 6 cups (1.4 L) distilled or purified water
- ½ cup (65 g) cornstarch
- 1 tablespoon (14 g) baking powder
- 1 tablespoon (15 ml) glycerin (Corn syrup may be substituted.)
- ½ cup (120 ml) blue Dawn or Joy dish detergent (Fairy, Dreft, or Yes also work well.)
- Large tray or bowl
- Compact disc (optional)

Bounce light waves create a rainbow of colors.

SAFETY TIPS AND HINTS

Use the recommended detergents for the best results. Bubbles will last longer on humid days when it's not too windy.

PROTOCOL

1 Light waves bend when they travel through substances such as glass, water, or bubbles. Fill a clear glass with water, put a pencil in the glass, and look at it from the side to observe this phenomeon, called refraction.

2 To make a giant bubble wand, tie one end of a long cotton string to the end of a long dowel or stick.

3 Put the string through a metal washer and tie it to the end of the other stick, leaving about 18 inches (46 cm) of string free, with the washer hanging in the middle.

4 Tie the end of the remaining free string to the end of the first stick, forming a string triangle. *Fig. 1.*

5 Mix the water and cornstarch. Add the remaining ingredients and mix well without whipping up tiny bubbles. Pour the bubble solution into a tray or larger bowl. *Fig. 2.*

6 Use the solution right away or let it sit for 15 minutes and stir gently before using.

7 With the two sticks together and the washer hanging down between, immerse the string on your bubble wand in the bubble mixture. Try not to tangle the string.

8 Draw the string up out of the bubble mixture and pull the sticks apart slowly to form a triangle, with a thin layer of bubble mix in the middle. *Fig. 3.*

9 Step backward or blow a bubble with your breath. You can "close" the bubbles by moving the sticks together to close the gap between strings. *Fig. 4.*

Fig. 1. Make a bubble wand.

Fig. 2. Mix up some bubble solution.

Fig. 3. Pull sticks and string apart to form a triangular film of bubble solution.

Fig. 4. Step back or blow to create a bubble.

How many colors do you see in the bubbles?

CREATIVE ENRICHMENT

Shine a flashlight onto a compact disc to make diffractions patterns on a wall.

THE PHYSICS BEHIND THE FUN

Water molecules like to stick together. Scientists call water's attractive, elastic tendency surface tension. Like a magnet, water molecules carry both positive and negative charges. Adding dish detergent to water allows you to blow bubbles by creating a thin film of water molecules sandwiched between two layers of soap molecules, all surrounding a large pocket of air. Glycerin and corn syrup slow down water evaporation, allowing bubbles to stick around longer.

Bubbles are usually round because the air pressure in a closed bubble is slightly higher than the air pressure outside of it. The forces of surface tension rearrange a bubble's molecular structure to have the least amount of surface area possible, and a sphere has the lowest surface area. Other forces, such as a breeze, can affect the shape of bubbles.

The thickness of the water and soap layer constantly changes. As the water evaporates, light waves hit the soap layers from many angles. Inside and outside of the bubble, light waves bend, bounce around, and interfere with each other (See Lab 6), giving the bubble a multitude of colors.

Michael Faraday b. 1791
ELECTROMAGNETIC INDUCTION

A SELF-TAUGHT STUDENT

Unlike many scientists of his time, Michael Faraday grew up in a family with almost no money or education. Michael had been born near London in 1791 and was the third of four children in his family. His father was a blacksmith. Because he had almost no formal schooling, Michael had to educate himself by reading books.

READING SCIENCE

Michael found himself surrounded by wonderful books when he went to work at the age of fourteen as an apprentice to a bookseller and bookbinder in London. He worked there until he was twenty, and he became interested in science. One of his favorite books was *Conversations on Chemistry*, written by a woman named Jane Marcet.

AN ENTHUSIASTIC ASSISTANT

When he stopped working at the book shop, Michael Faraday attended lectures given by well-known scientists. After listening to a series of science talks by the chemist Humphry Davy, he assembled his notes into a 300-page book and sent it to Davy. His initiative paid off, and Michael was hired to work in Davy's laboratory as an assistant.

IN THE LAB

In Davy's laboratory, Michael discovered two new chemical compounds containing the element chlorine. He also studied how gases move (diffuse) through the air and invented the first version of a piece of lab equipment called the Bunsen burner, which is still used in labs today. Michael was interested in producing glass for optical use, such as making lenses, and he produced a lens that later helped him to demonstrate that magnetism can affect rays of light.

ELECTRICITY AND MAGNETISM

Michael Faraday is most famous for his work studying the relationship between magnetism and electricity. His first experiment with electricity involved making a battery from coins, pieces of zinc, and salt water, but he moved on quickly from there. In 1821, Hans Christian Ørsted had described the relationship between electricity and magnets, called electromagnetism. Michael wanted to learn more about this fascinating marriage of physical forces.

MOTORS AND DUST EXPLOSIONS

By 1831, Faraday had demonstrated that when electrical current is run through a conductor, such as a metal wire, a magnetic field forms around the conducting material. He found that the opposite is also true: a magnet can be used to make an electrical current run through a wire. He called this phenomenon electromagnetic induction. Faraday used what he'd learned to invent some of the first electric motors using wires and magnets. He also studied dust explosions, designed lighthouses, worried about industrial pollution, and was an excellent science communicator who amazed audiences by filling soap bubbles with gases to demonstrate magnetism.

IN TODAY'S WORLD

Electromagnetic induction is still used in many motors and generators today.

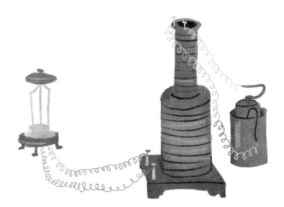

ELECTROMAGNETIC INDUCTION

Use a battery, a nail, and some wire to build an electromagnet.

MATERIALS

- Large nail (not stainless steel)
- Paper clips (metal, uncoated)
- Glasses or safety glasses
- Insulated copper wire (preferred), or 16 or 18 gauge copper wire
- Scissors
- Needle-nose pliers
- Electrical tape
- AA battery

SAFETY TIPS AND HINTS

Paper clips coated with plastic will not work for this project. It is best to use insulated wire for this project, to avoid burned fingers. The wire and battery will get hot, and the battery must be completely disconnected from the wires when you have completed the experiment. Follow the instructions carefully.

Fig. 7. See how many paper clips the magnet will lift.

PROTOCOL

1 Try to pick a paper clip up using a nail. Chances are, it will not work.

2 Put on glasses or safety glasses. To make the nail magnetic, cut a piece of copper wire six or seven times as long as a large nail. *Fig. 1.*

3 Coil the wire around the nail tightly, leaving enough wire on either end so that long pieces of wire extend from the top and bottom of the nail. *Fig. 2.*

4 Use needle-nose pliers or scissors to bend the ends of the wire into small loops. *Fig. 3.*

5 If not using insulated wire, wrap electrical tape around the wire extensions, leaving only the loops at either end exposed. *Fig. 4.*

6 Securely tape one loop onto one end of the battery using electrical tape. *Fig. 5.*

7 To magnetize the nail, close the circuit by grasping the taped portion of the free wire and touching the exposed loop to the open end of the battery. Now you have an electromagnet. *Fig. 6.*

8 Touch the magnetized nail to a paper clip to see whether you can pick it up.

9 Try to pick up more paper clips and record how many clips you can pick up with a single magnetized nail. *Fig. 7.*

CREATIVE ENRICHMENT

Repeat the experiment using nails made from different metals, different-sized wires, and different batteries to test how many paper clips you can lift at a time. Does the nail ever remain magnetized after the circuit has been disconnected? *Fig. 8.*

Fig. 1. Cut a piece of copper wire.

Fig. 2. Coil the wire around a nail, leaving uncoiled wire at both ends.

Fig. 3. Bend the ends of the wire into loops.

Fig. 4. Wrap insulation around the free wire.

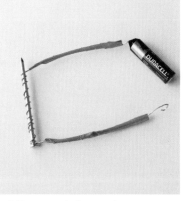

Fig. 5. Tape one wire loop to a battery.

Fig. 6. Close the circuit and use the nail to pick up a paper clip.

Fig. 8. Test whether the nail remains magnetized when the electrical current stops.

THE PHYSICS BEHIND THE FUN

Electrical force is produced when negatively charged subatomic particles called electrons flow from one place to another in a material called a conductor. Certain metals are good conductors.

As electrons flow from one area to another, they create a magnetic field. By running electrical current through a wire, it is possible to create a special magnet called an electromagnet. Coiling wire around a nail allows the current running through the wire to be transferred to the metal in the nail. The more times the wire is wrapped around the nail, the stronger the magnet will be.

Pierre Curie b. 1859
PIEZOELECTRICITY

A DAY DREAMER

Pierre Curie was a slow and thoughtful learner who loved to daydream. Born in Paris in 1859, he preferred exploring meadows and catching frogs and salamanders to traditional schooling. Mostly educated by his father, who was a physician, Pierre discovered a talent for math and geometry when he was a teenager.

THE SORBONNE

Pierre earned a degree in mathematics when he was sixteen years old, and he earned a master's degree in science from the famous Sorbonne University in Paris when he was eighteen. Lacking the money to continue his education, he went to work as a laboratory instructor. He and his brother Jacques had become interested in studying crystals when they learned that by heating crystals, one could produce electricity.

STRETCHING CRYSTALS

Pierre and Jacques suspected that when crystals were heated up, their geometry changed. They decided to test whether they could create electricity by simply changing the shape of crystals. Using tinfoil, glue, wire, and magnets, they stretched and squeezed different crystals, such as long, thin pieces of quartz, to see what would happen. The experiments proved that their theory was correct. Pierre and Jacques named the electrical current produced by stretching and squeezing crystals, piezoelectricity.

MAGNETISM

Pierre Curie was also interested in magnetism and how it was affected by temperature. Curie's Law, which he created, describes the effect of temperature on a phenomenon called paramagnetism. The Curie point, which he discovered, is the temperature at which magnetic materials such as iron stop being magnets.

A SHARED DREAM

While working on magnetism, Pierre met the brilliant scientist Marie Skłodowska. Like him, she had devoted her life to science. They married in 1895, the same year Pierre completed his doctoral degree. Marie was studying a new phenomenon, which she named radioactivity, using a piece of equipment invented by Pierre—a piezoelectric quartz electrometer. Together, they discovered two new radioactive elements, which they named polonium and radium. While Marie created chemical methods to purify radium, Pierre worked to characterize their amazing discovery. Both Pierre and Marie Curie hoped that their discoveries would make the world a better place.

A NOBEL PRIZE

Pierre was interested in the biological effects of radium and worked with physicians to develop radium therapy, which was the predecessor of radiation therapy. In 1903, Pierre and Marie were awarded the Nobel Prize in physics. Unfortunately, Pierre's work with radioactive materials was making him sick and weak. On a dark, rainy day in 1906, he accidentally stepped into the street in front of a horse-drawn wagon and was killed.

IN TODAY'S WORLD

Today, piezoelectricity is used to power everything from guitar amplifiers to light-up shoes.

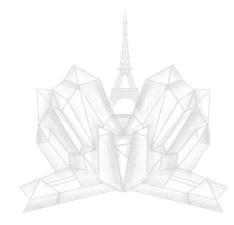

MINTY PIEZOELECTRIC CRYSTALS

Create a flash of blue light by crushing a mint with pliers.

MATERIALS

- Safety glasses
- Wintergreen mints, such as Lifesavers or Breath Savers
- Pliers or a hammer
- Plastic bin
- 27mm piezo discs with leads for microphone, drum, acoustic pickup, guitar (optional)
- Small LED (optional)
- 2 alligator clip test leads (optional)

SAFETY TIPS AND HINTS

Always wear safety glasses when crushing mints to avoid eye injury. Certain mints work better than others for creating a flash of light.

PROTOCOL

1 Put on safety glasses.

2 Place your mints and pliers in a plastic bin.

3 Find a room dark enough to make a faint flash of light visible.

4 With the lights on, position the mint in the teeth of the pliers.

5 Turn the lights off and crush the mint. Watch for a flash of light. *Fig. 1 and Fig. 2.*

6 If you didn't see a flash, try it again.

7 Compare different mints to see which work best.

Fig. 1. Use pliers to crush the mints.

THE PHYSICS BEHIND THE FUN

Crystals, such as diamonds, salt, quartz, and sugar, are solid networks of repeating molecules. As Pierre Curie discovered, squeezing or stretching crystals causes negatively charged particles called electrons to move around and make an electrical current, called piezoelectricity. Piezoelectricity causes certain crystals to emit light when crushed. Scientists call this triboluminescence.

Scientists think that chomping on candy causes tiny piezoelectrical currents to interact with nitrogen gas in the air. This energetic interaction produces triboluminescence in the form of ultraviolet light, which is invisible to human eyes. Mints are special though. In addition to sugar, they often contain certain chemical flavors such as wintergreen. When crushed, the minty chemicals interact with piezoelectricity and nitrogen to produce flashes of visible blue light.

A small piece of mint is easier to crush.

Fig. 2. Watch for a flash of blue light.

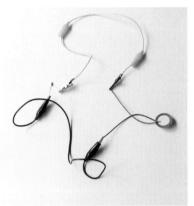

Fig. 3. Set up an electrical circuit using an LED and a piezo disk.

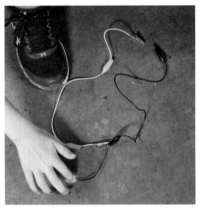

Fig. 4. In a dark room, tap the piezo disc strongly with your fingernail.

Fig. 5. If the LED doesn't flash when you tap the disc, switch the clips on the LED and try again.

CREATIVE ENRICHMENT

To use a piezo disc to produce enough energy to light an LED: Clip an alligator test lead securely to the metal on each of the piezo disc test leads. Clip the opposite end of each lead to one of the LED wires. Go into a room that can be darkened and set the disc on a flat surface. Turn off the lights and strongly tap the LED disc with your pointer finger or fingernail. Be sure that you're not touching the metal on the alligator clips. If everything is connected correctly, you should see faint flashes of light from the LED. If the LED doesn't flash when you apply pressure, turn on the light, switch the clips on the LED leads to change the polarity, turn off the light, and try it again. *Fig. 3 – Fig. 5.*

Lise Meitner b. 1878
NUCLEAR FISSION

VIENNA

Lise Meitner was born in 1878 in Vienna, a large city that was then in the multinational state of Austria-Hungary. The third of eight children, she had four sisters and three brothers. Lise's family was Jewish, and her father was a lawyer. Although they valued education, at that time girls were not allowed to pursue an education beyond primary (grade) school. When Lise was eight years old, she kept a notebook of her observations. She wrote about the rainbow of colors she saw in a thin film of oil and about the reflection of light. It was the beginning of her love of science and math.

A TOUGH EXAM

In 1901, women were finally allowed to take an entrance exam at the University of Vienna. Cramming the eight years of education she had missed into two years, Lise was one of few women admitted to the school. In college, she developed an interest in physics and became the second woman to earn a doctoral degree at the university.

ATOMIC WOMAN

A talented researcher, Dr. Meitner studied radioactivity. Some of her experiments involved sending beams of radioactive particles into metal foil, such as aluminum foil. She was surprised to find that the higher the atomic mass of the metal in the foil was, the more the radioactive particles scattered when they hit it. Her work later helped a man named Ernest Rutherford determine the structure of atoms.

A COLLEAGUE

Lise Meitner moved to Berlin, Germany, which was called Prussia back then. She attended lectures by the famous physicist Max Planck and did research with a scientist named Otto Hahn. Women were not allowed at the research institute where she worked, so she had to work in a woodshop, which served as her laboratory, and use the bathroom at a restaurant down the street. Otto Hahn was made a professor, but Meitner was not paid for her work. After a few years, things got better. She became friends with several physicists at the institute, but she was never paid as well as Otto.

AN ESCAPE

As an adult, Lise converted to the Christian religion, but World War II put her in grave danger because of her Jewish heritage. Otto Hahn helped her escape to Sweden, where she was safe. Sadly, all her equipment was in Germany and she could not continue her research in person. Hahn continued to send her his experimental results, which suggested that the nucleus of an element called uranium could be split.

A REVELATION

Although Hahn could not decipher how a nucleus could split apart, Lise figured it out. While walking through wintery Swedish woods with her nephew, she imagined a droplet of water splitting in half—like a dividing cell. Lisa pulled out a piece of paper and did the mathematical calculations. They added up. She wrote to Hahn and they both published papers on the phenomenon, which Meitner called fission. Otto Hahn was awarded a Nobel Prize for their discovery, but Lise Meitner was left out and got nothing. Eventually she won many other prizes for her work. Dr. Meitner hoped that her discovery would be used for good, rather than for destruction.

IN TODAY'S WORLD

Nuclear reactors use uranium as fuel to create controlled fission reactions that produce energy without burning fossil fuels.

NUCLEAR FISSION MODEL

Make slime and use it to create a model of Lise Meitner's liquid droplet model of nuclear fission.

MATERIALS

- 1 bottle (5 fl oz or 147 ml) clear, washable glue, glow-in-the-dark glue, or white glue
- 1 teaspoon (5 g) baking soda
- Food coloring (optional)
- Contact lens solution containing boric acid or sodium borate as a preservative
- Several small, identical objects, such as beads or sculpting clay rolled into balls

SAFETY TIPS AND HINTS

Contact lens solution lacking boric acid or sodium borate will not work. Boric acid in contact lens solution combines with baking soda to make borate, a crosslinking chemical that makes the long chemical chains in glue stick together. To make clear slime, place slime made from clear glue in a sealed container or plastic bag for a few days to allow air bubbles to escape.

PROTOCOL

1 Place around 5 oz (147 ml) glue into a bowl.

2 Stir in the baking soda and mix well. Add food coloring, if desired.

3 Mix in 3 teaspoons (15 ml) of contact lens solution, stirring until the slime is no longer sticky and can be rolled into a ball. *Fig. 1 and Fig. 2.*

Fig. 3. Put a few small objects in the slime to represent neutrons.

4 Shape the slime into a single round ball to represent the nucleus of an atom. Push three or more small objects into the slime to represent subatomic particles called neutrons. Roll the slime into a neat ball again to represent the unstable nucleus of an atom. *Fig. 3.*

Push a small object representing an extra, destabilizing neutron into the ball of slime.

5 Sculpt the slime into an egg shape to represent an unstable nucleus. *Fig. 4.*

6 Use your thumb and finger to narrow the center of the egg-shaped slime. Pull the two sides apart and stretch the slime to distort the nucleus into two equal parts. *Fig. 5.*

7 Pinch the center of the slime to break the two pieces apart and roll them into individual balls, representing nuclear fission. *Fig. 6.*

8 Extract three of the neutrons from the slime to represent neutrons released during nuclear fission. When nuclear fission occurs, an enormous amount of energy is released as well. *Fig. 7.*

Fig. 1. Add contact lens solution into slime mixture and stir.

Fig. 2. Mix until the slime is no longer sticky and can be rolled into a ball.

Fig. 7. Extract neutrons from the slime to represent neutrons ejected during nuclear fission.

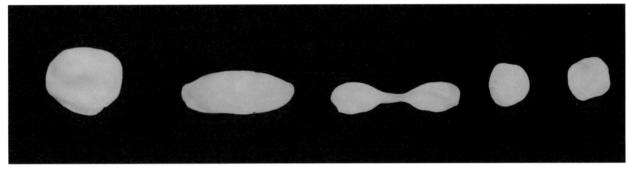

Fig. 4, 5, 6. Sculpt the slime from a ball . . .   into an elongated shape . . .   into to a shape pinched in the center . . .   into two distinct balls.

CREATIVE ENRICHMENT

Observe the droplet surface tension of water by adding a single drop of water to a piece of plastic wrap to see how it holds together. How many drops of water can you drip onto a penny before the surface tension is finally broken?

Observe surface tension by dripping water on a penny. How many drops will a single penny hold?

THE PHYSICS BEHIND THE FUN

The nucleus of an atom is the dense, central portion that is made up of sub-atomic particles called protons, which have a positive charge, and neutrons, which carry no charge. Normally, atoms are stable and do not break apart. However, certain atoms containing large numbers of protons and neutrons can split in two, spontaneously or artificially, in a process called nuclear fission.

Lise Meitner based her model of nuclear fission on the liquid droplet model. The droplet model imagines that the surface of an atom's nucleus is held together by forces like the ones on the surface of a water droplet. Dr. Meitner realized that in certain unstable atoms, these forces could be disrupted to cause the atom to split into two smaller nuclei carrying lots of energy.

In this lab, slime allows you to illustrate nuclear fission. You can see how a single unstable element bombarded with a particle called a neutron can cause an atom to split in the process of fission. The neutron is captured, the unstable nucleus elongates and distorts, and finally the atom splits in two, ejecting more neutrons in the process.

Albert Einstein b. 1879
RELATIVITY

MUSIC LOVER

Albert Einstein was born in Ulm, Germany in 1879. His father was an engineer and a salesman. Their family moved frequently, first to Italy and then to Switzerland. As a child, Albert was particularly good at math and physics, but he also loved music and played the violin very well. Later in life he would say "I often think in music" and claimed that if he were not a physicist, he would have been a musician.

NATURE AS MATH

Albert was a creative thinker and did not like formal education, which was based on memorizing facts. He saw nature as a mathematical structure and was always thinking about how to answer questions he had about the universe. Although he had trained as a teacher, Albert couldn't find a job. In 1901, he became a Swiss citizen and went to work at the Swiss Patent Office, where he examined new inventions.

A MIRACLE YEAR

While working at the patent office, Albert used math and experimentation to explore scientific ideas that interested him. In 1905, he published four papers that would change science forever. One described the photoelectric effect, supporting the idea that light was made of energetic particles he named *quanta*, which traveled in waves. The second explained Brownian motion, which is the random motion of particles in a liquid or gas. Another paper introduced his theory of special relativity, merging Newton's mechanics (Lab 3) and electromagnetism (Lab 8). Finally, he studied the relationship between gravity, space, and time and developed what is called the general theory of relativity. In this work, he introduced what he called mass–energy equivalence, which gave rise to the famous equation $E = MC^2$ (energy = mass × the speed of light.)

BENDING LIGHT

In 1914, Einstein moved back to Germany to become the director of the Kaiser Wilhelm Physical Institute. In 1903, he married the physicist Mileva Mari, whom some historians believe contributed to his work on special relativity, but he divorced her in 1919. In 1916, Albert introduced his theory of general relativity, which attributes the gravitational attraction between masses to the warping of space and time between those masses. He correctly predicted that the light from a star would be bent by the sun's gravity.

A NOBEL PRIZE

Albert Einstein was awarded a Nobel Prize for Physics in 1921. However, it was for his work on the photoelectric effect rather than his groundbreaking theory of general relativity. At that time, anti-Jewish sentiment, called antisemitism, was building in the world. Einstein continued to work on the problems of physics, but he fled Germany to live in the United States in 1933 when Adolf Hitler came into power.

AMERICA

Einstein became a professor at Princeton University in New Jersey. Albert worried about his friends in Europe as Hitler's anti-intellectual (anti-education) movement took hold and Germans targeted Jews and universities. Albert Einstein played a role in convincing the United States to create the nuclear weapons that eventually brought World War II to an end, but he hated war. Einstein also hated racism and called it America's "worst disease." He died in 1955, when he was seventy-six years old.

IN TODAY'S WORLD

Albert Einstein's theory of general relativity proved to be correct, and it has helped modern scientists understand phenomena such as black holes, where the gravitational attraction between masses is so enormous that even light cannot escape.

PLAYGROUND BALL RELATIVITY

Use a picnic blanket and playground balls to observe how massive objects bend space.

MATERIALS

- Picnic blanket or old sheet
- Large ball, such as a soccer ball or basketball
- Several smaller balls, such as tennis balls, hand balls, and golf balls

SAFETY TIPS AND HINTS

This lab works best with at least four people to hold the blanket or sheet.

PROTOCOL

1 With at least three other people, hold a blanket or sheet as flat and level as possible. It should be parallel to the ground. *Fig. 1.*

2 Roll a large ball into the center of the blanket. Observe the blanket near the ball. *Fig. 2.*

3 One at a time, place the smaller balls on the blanket. Do they stay in place or roll toward the larger ball? *Fig. 3 and Fig. 4.*

4 Use the blanket to throw the balls up in the air and try to catch them with the blanket. Think about the force acting on the balls as they are propelled upwards and fall back down toward Earth. *Fig. 5 and Fig. 6.*

Fig. 6. Think about the physical forces acting on the balls as they move up and down.

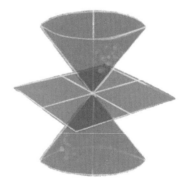

Fig. 1. Hold a sheet or blanket level.

Fig. 2. Roll a large ball to the center and observe how the fabric is bent by its mass (weight).

Fig. 3. Place smaller balls on the edges of the blanket.

Fig. 4. Test balls of different sizes and mass (weight.)

Fig. 5. Toss the balls into the air and catch them with the fabric.

CREATIVE ENRICHMENT

Try this experiment on a trampoline with a person standing in the middle. Do the balls roll toward where the person is standing?

THE PHYSICS BEHIND THE FUN

Albert Einstein visualized time and space knitted together into a fabric, like the blanket used in this experiment. His theory of general relativity stated that that massive bodies, such as stars and planets, create warps and curves in the flexible fabric of space and time, in much the same way that a heavy ball bends the fabric of your blanket.

The sun is a massive star at the center of our solar system. Earth and the other planets orbiting the sun are far less massive and follow curves created by the sun in the spatial fabric. The project in this lab helps illustrate this, as smaller balls on a blanket roll toward the area where the weight of the larger ball bends the fabric.

Balls thrown up into the air are pulled back down by gravity—the same force that attracts the moon to the Earth and the planets to the sun!

Katharine Burr Blodgett b. 1898
FILMS

LEARNING FRENCH

Katharine Burr Blodgett was born in 1898. Katharine's father, a patent attorney in Schenectady, New York, was shot to death during a robbery shortly before her birth. Her mother moved with Katherine and her brother to Paris, France, when they were young. She wanted her children to learn a second language.

SCHOOL IN AMERICA

After going back and forth between New York and Europe for several years, Katharine finally started school when she was eight years old. She did well at her studies and got a scholarship to Bryn Mawr College, where she was inspired by her math professor Charlotte Angas Scott and her physics professor James Barnes. After college, she went to the University of Chicago to get her master's degree. While she was there, Katharine studied gas masks to learn how different materials adsorbed (attached to) gases.

GENERAL ELECTRIC

Katharine went to work at General Electric, where she worked in the lab of Irving Langmuir for six years before going to Cambridge University in England to get her doctoral degree. One of very few women at Cambridge, she studied with the famous physicist Ernest Rutherford and became the first woman to earn a doctoral degree in physics from the university.

THIN FILMS

Returning to General Electric, Dr. Katharine Blodgett resumed the work she had been doing with Irving Langmuir. Interested in designing techniques for applying thin films of fluids on surfaces such as glass and metal, she refined a piece of equipment called the Langmuir-Blodgett trough. The pan-like apparatus* allowed her to float oily substances on water, and she used them to coat glass and metal. Some of the layers she created were a single molecule thick.

INVISIBLE GLASS

By adding layer after layer of non-reflective coating to glass until she had forty-four thin layers, Katharine created glass with no reflection, which proved extremely useful. Her non-reflective glass was used for movie cameras, telescopes, non-reflective eyeglasses, and submarine periscopes and spy cameras during World War II.

A CREATIVE MIND

Katharine Burr Blodgett won many awards and was inducted into the National Inventors Hall of Fame. Besides non-reflective glass, she invented a "color ruler" that allowed scientists to measure the thickness of thin layers and a device to measure humidity. Katharine was a conservationist and an actress in her local theater, and she loved gardening. She also liked playing cards, writing funny poetry, and looking through telescopes. Dr. Burr Blodgett died in 1979.

IN TODAY'S WORLD

Katharine Burr Blodget's thin-film technique, which creates Langmuir-Blodgett (LB) films, is used to make computer components and anti-reflective glass, among other things.

*The design of the Langmuir-Blodgett (LB) trough was inspired by an apparatus designed by Agnes Pockels, a relatively unknown scientist who did early, important work on surface tension and thin films. Pockels is one of the scientists featured in *Chemistry for Kids* in the Kitchen Pantry Scientist series.

THIN FILMS

Use a thin film of clear nail polish to make iridescent rainbow paper.

MATERIALS

- Clear nail polish
- Scissors
- Disposable plastic container, such as a recyclable food take-out container. (A 5- x 8-inch [13- x 20-cm] container works well for this project.)
- Black construction paper or card stock cut into squares or rectangles slightly smaller than the container
- Other colors of construction paper or card stock (optional)
- Disposable gloves (optional)

SAFETY TIPS AND HINTS

Do this project outdoors or in a well-ventilated area to avoid inhaling nail polish fumes. Lay down newspaper to protect surfaces from nail polish. Add the paper to the floating nail polish right away, before the polish has time to dry.

It may take some practice to perfect your technique.

PROTOCOL

1 Pour 1 inch (2.5 cm) or so of water into a disposable container. *Fig. 1.*

2 Put a single drop of clear nail polish in the center of the water and observe the film that spreads over the surface. *Fig. 2.*

3 Immediately, place a piece of paper in the center of the film and push the paper down to the bottom of the container with one finger. The edges of the film will probably wrap around the edges. *Fig. 3.*

4 Carefully pull the paper out and turn it over to see how well the film covered it. *Fig. 4.*

5 Put the rainbow paper on a piece of paper towel or newspaper to dry. *Fig. 5.*

6 Between pieces of rainbow paper, use scrap paper to "sweep" the water's surface clean of any extra nail polish.

Fig. 1. Pour an inch (2.5 cm) or so of water into a disposable container.

Fig. 2. Put a single drop of clear nail polish in the center of the water.

Fig. 3. Place a piece of paper on the surface and push it down to the bottom.

Fig. 4. After a few seconds, remove the paper from the water.

Fig. 5. Dry your project on a paper towel.

CREATIVE ENRICHMENT

Use this thin-film technique to make bookmarks. See what happens when you add multiple layers to a single piece of paper.

THE PHYSICS BEHIND THE FUN

Fingernail polish is less dense than water, which allows it to float. It is made up of a chemical called nitrocellulose, which can form very thin films. The nitrocellulose is dissolved in chemicals called solvents to keep the nail polish sticky. Once it has been spread out in a thin layer, the solvents evaporate quickly in the air and the nail polish hardens into a shiny material. When you put a drop of clear nail polish on water, it immediately spreads out in a thin film that dries very quickly.

In this lab, the polish is spread out in a thin layer on paper. The clear film is thick in some areas and thin in others. As light travels through the film, the light waves are reflected and refracted (bent). As a result, they interfere with each other and produce a rainbow of colors, depending on the thickness of the film. See Labs 6 and 7 to learn more about light and color.

Cecilia Payne-Gaposchkin b. 1900
STAR MATERIAL

A LIBRARY

Cecilia Payne was born in Wendover in Buckinghamshire, England. Her father died when she was only four, leaving her mother to raise Cecilia and her two siblings. The family was financially well-off and had a large library, where Cecilia read literature and learned about music and theater. They moved to London when she was twelve, so her brother could go to a better school.

AN EDUCATION

Cecilia's talent for music led the well-known composer Gustav Holst to encourage her to make a career of it. She loved science more than music, though, and she won a scholarship to Newnham College, a women's college at Cambridge University. At that time, few women studied science and they had to sit at the front of lecture halls, enduring the teasing of male students. Cecilia kept her focus and completed her studies there, although at the time, Cambridge did not award degrees to women.

STARS IN HER EYES

Cecilia became fascinated with the stars while attending a lecture by a man named Arthur Eddington. He spoke about photographing stars off the coast of Africa in 1919 during a total eclipse of the sun to test Albert Einstein's (Lab 11) theory of relativity. She was so excited about his lecture that she almost had a nervous breakdown.

STELLAR RESEARCH

In 1923, Cecilia moved to the United States to work with the astronomer Harlow Shapley at the Harvard Observatory. She spent the next two years working day and night to analyze thousands of images from the observatory's collection of stellar spectra, which contained the light signatures from stars. Cecilia combined the data she interpreted from the collection with a new theory developed by Meghnad Saha, a scientist from India, and came up with a revolutionary theory of her own—that the sun is made mostly of hydrogen and that helium is the second most plentiful element.

A BRILLIANT THESIS

When Cecilia showed her work to Harlow Shapley and his colleague Henry Norris Russell, they rejected her conclusion, siding with the current theory that the sun had the same elemental composition as Earth. She published her thesis, but downplayed her discovery as possibly incorrect, and became the first woman to earn a doctoral degree in astronomy from Harvard. It was not until Russell came to the same conclusion himself years later that people accepted that the sun was made of hydrogen and helium. Russell was congratulated for "his" discovery, while Cecilia got no credit until decades later.

A TRAILBLAZER

Despite the sexism she faced, Dr. Cecilia Payne forged ahead with her research, studying highly luminous (bright) stars and trying to understand the structure of the Milky Way. She married a Russian astronomer named Sergei Gaposchkin and added his last name to hers. They had three children who spent many hours in the observatory, because Harvard didn't pay them enough for them to be able to afford childcare. In 1956, Cecilia was finally given a faculty position and became the first female professor of the Harvard Faculty in Arts and Sciences and the first woman to head a department at Harvard. Besides writing five books, she has an asteroid named for her and won a constellation of awards before she died in 1979.

IN TODAY'S WORLD

Every object in the universe reflects, absorbs, or produces light waves. Spectroscopy is a technique that uses a prism or grooves to split light waves from an object, such as a star, into its different wavelengths. The technique is one of the most powerful tools used by astronomers today to study what stars are made of.

SOLAR SPECTRUM

Use a compact disc to observe the sun's spectrum in a cardboard box.

MATERIALS

- Sharp pencil or pen
- Large cardboard box
- White paper
- Compact disc
- Flashlight (optional)
- Makeup (magnifying) mirror (optional)
- Camera, such as one on a phone

SAFETY TIPS AND HINTS

This project works well in the morning or late afternoon when the sun is at a low angle. Do not reflect sunlight back into your own eyes.

PROTOCOL

1 Use a sharp pencil or pen to poke a small hole in the center of one side of a cardboard box.

2 Cover the bottom of the box and the three sides of the box without the hole with white paper.

3 Hold the box so the light travels through the small hole to make a bright, focused dot on the bottom of the box or the side of the box opposite the pinhole. You may have to adjust the angle of the box. *Fig. 1.*

4 Place a compact disc so that its edge is in the dot of light, or just in front of it. *Fig. 2.*

5 Play with the angle of the disc until you separate out the visible spectrum of light coming from the sun into a rainbow. *Fig. 3.*

6 When you have spread the colors out as much as possible, photograph the solar spectrum you created.

7 Use the compact disc and sunlight to create more rainbows inside of the box. *Fig. 4, Fig. 5.*

Fig. 6. Use a curved mirror to refocus the pinhole of light in the box and use the compact disc to spread out the solar spectra.

CREATIVE ENRICHMENT

Use a concave mirror to refocus the pinhole of light inside the box. Then, use the compact disc to make more solar spectra on the bottom and sides of the box. Take photographs of the spectra. *Fig. 6.*

Create a spectrograph with the light from a flashlight. Compare it to the solar spectrograph.

Fig. 1. Hold the box so sunlight travels through the hole.

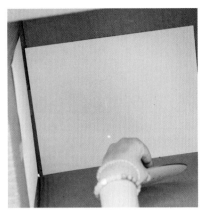

Fig. 2. Set a compact disc just in front of the point of light.

Fig. 3. Spread the colors of sunlight out.

Fig. 4. Use the compact disc to create more colorful patterns in the box.

Fig. 5. Photograph the patterns you create.

THE PHYSICS BEHIND THE FUN

In this lab, you use the series of grooves in a compact disc to create a colorful solar spectrum. Each tiny groove produces a diffraction pattern (see Lab 7). The light from each groove interferes with the light from neighboring grooves. As a result, each color is intensified at particular angles, producing the rainbow spectrum you observe.

When chemical elements interact with light, they leave a fingerprint. Every celestial object has a light signature, called a spectrum, made up of these fingerprints. In spectroscopy, a device called a spectrograph channels light coming into a telescope through a tiny hole or slit to isolate light from a single area or object, such as a star.

The light is then bounced off a special grating, splitting the light into its different wavelengths so that the fractured light can be observed and recorded (see Labs 3, 6, and 7).

Around 1875, a British astronomy enthusiast named Margaret Huggins figured out how to capture the spectra of stars in photographs. Astronomers studied the light patterns and compared them to those of known chemicals to guess what stars are made of. Studying solar spectrographs allowed Cecilia Payne to correctly conclude that hydrogen and helium are the sun's most abundant elements.

Mary Golda Ross b. 1908
AEROSPACE ENGINEERING

GREAT GRANDDAUGHTER OF A CHIEF

Mary Golda Ross was born in Park Hill, Oklahoma in 1908. The second of five children, she was the great granddaughter of John Ross, who had been the chief of the Cherokee nation from 1828 to 1866. Despite the best efforts of Indigenous leaders such as John Ross, the United States government had forcibly removed a hundred thousand Native Americans from their land and resettled them in Oklahoma in a deadly, devastating march from their homes known as "The Trail of Tears."

TAHLEQUAH

Mary was extremely bright, and she was happy to be brought up in the Cherokee tradition of equal education for boys and girls. Her parents sent her to live with her grandparents in Tahlequah, the capitol of the Cherokee Nation, which stood beside the foothills of the Ozark Mountains. When she turned sixteen, Mary went to Northeastern State Teachers College in Tahlequah, where she earned her bachelor's degree in mathematics.

THE GREAT DEPRESSION

During the Great Depression, Mary taught math and science at a school out in the countryside. After teaching for nine years, she went to work at the Bureau of Indian Affairs in Washington, D.C. and then at an American Indian boarding school in Santa Fe, New Mexico. In 1938, Mary moved to Colorado to get a master's degree in mathematics. While she was in school there, she took as many astronomy classes as she could.

THE WAR

When World War II broke out, Mary moved to California to work for Lockheed, an American aerospace company. Her job included studying the effects of air pressure on fighter jets and water pressure on submarine-launched vehicles. Mary was so smart and talented that in 1952 she was made part of a top-secret think tank called "skunkworks" in which she was the only woman and the only Native American.

A ROCKET SCIENTIST

After the war, Mary studied aerospace engineering as she continued to work on designing satellites and rockets. She was part of the Space Race, which aimed to send humans out of Earth's orbit. At Lockheed, Mary helped write NASA's Planetary Flight Handbook, a guide to space travel. She believed that women would make great astronauts, although she added "I'd rather stay down here and analyze the data."

AN INSPIRING FIGURE

Mary Golda Ross eventually became a senior advanced systems staff engineer at Lockheed. When she retired, Mary spoke at schools, encouraging young women and Indigenous youths to consider careers in technology and engineering. At the age of ninety-six, she participated in the opening ceremonies for the National Museum of the American Indian in Washington D.C. Her image can be found on the 2019 one-dollar coin, along with that of American Indian astronaut John Herrington, whom her work helped launch into space in 2002.

IN TODAY'S WORLD

The work of Mary Golda Ross and her colleagues is engrained in today's aerospace industry, from rocket designs to satellites.

HIGH-FLYING WATER ROCKET

Send a plastic bottle flying sky-high by adding some water and then pumping air into the bottle until you have liftoff.

MATERIALS

- Cardboard box, such as a shoebox
- 1.5-liter plastic bottle
- Wine cork cut in half that fits in the mouth of your bottle
- Needle for inflating balls
- Bicycle or ball pump
- Safety glasses

SAFETY TIPS AND HINTS

An adult should cut the cork in half with a serrated knife. Wear eye protection and make sure that everyone is behind the rocket before you launch.

PROTOCOL

1 Cut a notch in the side of a box to create a launch pad to hold a 1.5-liter bottle in place, upside down, at a 45-degree angle.

2 Push a ball inflation needle through half of a cork until it pokes out of the opposite side. It may help to use the hole from a corkscrew as a guide. *Fig. 1.*

3 Fill the plastic bottle with water until it is about one-third full and insert the cork in the bottle.

4 Attach the needle to the bike pump. *Fig. 2.*

Fig. 6. As the water shoots down, the rocket shoots up!

5 Put on your safety glasses. Set the bottle, cork-side down, in the cardboard box so that the bottom of the bottle is pointing up and away from you at approximately a 45-degree angle. *Fig. 3.*

6 Standing behind the launch pad, pump air into the bottle. The air pressure will build in the bubble at the top of the rocket. When the pressure gets high enough, it will force the cork and water out of the bottom of the bottle with lots of force. As the water shoots down, the rocket will shoot up! *Fig. 4 – Fig. 6.*

CREATIVE ENRICHMENT

Launch the rocket using more water—or less water—to see how it affects the rocket's flight.

Fig. 1. Push a ball inflation needle through half a cork.

Fig. 2. Attach the needle to a bike pump.

Fig. 3. Set the bottle, cork-side down, in a cardboard box, pointing up and away from you.

Fig. 4. Start pumping air into the bottle

Fig. 5. When the air pressure is high enough, it will force the cork and water out of the bottle.

THE PHYSICS BEHIND THE FUN

Three important physical forces act on rockets launched from Earth: thrust, drag, and weight. Thrust pushes a rocket up and away from its launch point, while drag from air resistance slows it down. Weight, the third important force, is produced by gravity, which pulls down on the mass of the rocket. With a good background in math and science, engineers can figure out how to maximize a vehicle's thrust, while minimizing its drag and weight.

NASA's rockets use rocket fuel for thrust, but a bottle rocket like the one in this lab uses water. As pressurized air forces the water out of your rocket, the rocket moves in the opposite direction, just like Sir Isaac Newton's (Lab 3) Third Law says it will, when it states, "For every action, there is an equal and opposite reaction."

Luis Walter Alvarez b. 1911
BUBBLE CHAMBER

MIDWESTERN EDUCATION

Luis Walter Alvarez was born in San Francisco in 1911. When he was fifteen, his family moved to Rochester, Minnesota, where his father was a physician at the Mayo Clinic. Although he had always planned to go to college at the University of California, Berkeley, Luis went to the University of Chicago instead. There he earned his bachelors, masters, and doctoral degrees. Luis's advisor was Nobel Prize–winning scientist Arthur Compton.

COSMIC RAYS

While studying at the University of Chicago, Luis made a "telescope" out of Geiger tubes, which could detect radioactivity. He was interested in studying cosmic rays, which are made up of high-energy particles traveling through space and into Earth's atmosphere. Luis concluded from the data he collected that primary cosmic rays which had not collided with the gases in Earth's atmosphere were mostly positively charged.

RADIATION LABORATORY

After Chicago, Dr. Alvarez moved to Berkeley, California to work with the well-known nuclear physicist Ernest Lawrence. Lawrence was famous for his work on the atom and was about to win a Nobel Prize for his invention of the cyclotron, which created streams of fast-moving charged particles by accelerating them along a spiral pathway. While at the Radiation Laboratory at Berkeley, Alvarez figured out how to use the cyclotron to study particles called neutrons, which reside in the nucleus of atoms.

RADAR

World War II found Luis Alvarez in England, training the British to use new radar technology he had helped develop while working at MIT, the Massachusetts Institute of Technology. He then returned to the United States to work with Robert Oppenheimer on the Manhattan Project. Luis helped design "Fat Man," a plutonium bomb detonated over Nagasaki, Japan in 1945, destroying the city in a horrific nuclear explosion. Alvarez flew on a plane called *The Great Artist*, which flew in formation with the planes dropping the two atomic bombs on Japan to measure the force of the explosions.

BUBBLE CHAMBER

After the war, Luis became a professor at University of California–Berkeley and worked on improving the cyclotron. He also created a new type of "bubble chamber" that could be used to detect new kinds of particles and to study particle interactions and behavior. The seven-foot (213 cm)-long bubble chamber had a metal frame and glass walls that allowed for photography. Liquid hydrogen inside the chamber could be heated so particles passing through the hydrogen would make the hydrogen boil, leaving a signature marked by a path of bubbles. Alvarez won the 1968 Nobel Prize in Physics for this work.

BALLOONS, PYRAMIDS, AND DINOSAURS

Luis Walter Alvarez loved piloting airplanes. He helped develop high-altitude particle sensors carried by balloons and aircraft. Alvarez also traveled to Egypt to search for hidden chambers in the great pyramids using the signatures of muons, particles produced by cosmic rays colliding with the atmosphere. Luis and his geologist son wrote a paper providing evidence that the dinosaurs went extinct as the result of an extraterrestrial object colliding with Earth, which proved to be correct. Alvarez died in 1988.

IN TODAY'S WORLD

Alvarez's work helped to build a foundation for particle physics and modern cosmology, which is the study of the origin and development of the universe.

CLOUD CHAMBER

Build a cloud chamber to observe the signature trails left by subatomic particles such as muons.

MATERIALS

- Black paper
- Scissors
- Glass jar with a metal lid or a plastic jar, such as a peanut butter jar
- Felt or sponge
- Chewing gum or sculpting clay (optional)
- Safety glasses and protective gloves
- 90% rubbing alcohol (isopropanol)
- Dry ice
- Small container that can be filled with warm water and set on the jar
- Rimmed container, such as a casserole dish, large enough to hold dry ice and the jar
- Flashlight
- Stopwatch (optional)

SAFETY TIPS AND HINTS

- Adult supervision required. Wear glasses or safety glasses. Dry ice can cause burns and must be handled only with gloves. Do this project in a well-ventilated area. You will need a room that can be darkened to see the subatomic particles passing through the chamber.
- We have had the best luck using jars with metal lids.
- Watch a video of vapor trails in the cloud chamber we made while photographing this book to see what to look for when your chamber is complete. (The Kitchen Pantry Scientist video channel: youtu.be/f4ki9YNuvLk.)

PROTOCOL

1 Cut out a piece of black paper to fit securely inside of a jar lid, so that the lid will still close.

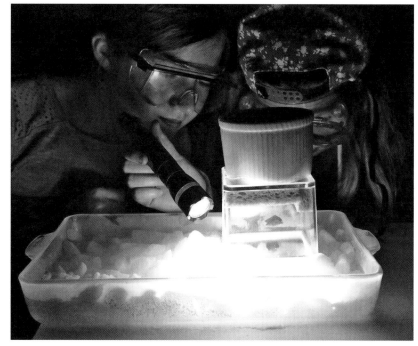

Fig. 5. Wait several minutes, turn off the lights, and shine a flashlight beam from the side onto the dark paper at the bottom of the jar.

2 Cut a sponge or some felt so it is slightly bigger than the inside of a jar and can be jammed in tightly. Put the sponge in the bottom of the jar and use chewing gum or sculpting clay to secure it to the jar, if needed. Check that it doesn't fall out when you turn it upside down. *Fig. 1.*

3 Put on safety glasses. Soak the sponge or felt in the jar with enough rubbing alcohol (isopropyl) that it is wet, but not dripping. Extra alcohol can be poured off, if necessary. *Fig. 2.*

4 Tighten the lid on the jar.

5 Wearing gloves, cover the bottom of a rimmed container with dry ice.

6 Take the dry-ice container to a room that can be darkened. Turn the jar upside down and place it on the dry ice. *Fig. 3.*

7 Fill a small container with warm water and set it on top of the jar. Wait a few minutes so that the temperature difference inside the jar causes a vapor of evaporated alcohol and water to form. *Fig. 4.*

8 Turn off the lights and shine a flashlight beam into the cloud chamber from the side onto the paper on the jar's bottom. After several minutes, when you look at the black paper, the vapor in the jar will resemble impossibly tiny flakes of falling snow. The light will illuminate tiny clouds called vapor trails formed by subatomic particles passing through the alcohol vapors in the chamber. *Fig. 5.*

9 Each type of particle creates a signature type of vapor trail. How many do you see? *Fig. 6. and Fig. 7.*

Fig. 1. Cut a sponge to fit tightly in the bottom of a jar.

Fig. 2. Soak the sponge with rubbing alcohol.

Fig. 3. Turn the jar upside down and place it on dry ice.

Fig. 4. Fill a small container with warm water and set it on top of the jar.

Fig. 6. Vapor trails

Fig. 7. Vapor trails

CREATIVE ENRICHMENT

Use a stopwatch to count how many particles you observe per minute. Molecules in the atmosphere interact with subatomic particles bombarding us from space. Think about why your cloud chamber would encounter more particles if you set it up on a tall mountain, or in an airplane.

THE PHYSICS BEHIND THE FUN

There are invisible high-energy particles and waves, called radiation, all around us. Most radiation humans encounter is relatively harmless and is called background radiation. Some radiation is emitted from radioactive substances on Earth, such as uranium rocks and radon gas. Other radiation, such as ultraviolet light from the sun, comes from space. Luckily, the Earth's magnetic fields shield us from most cosmic radiation.

The cloud chamber you make in this lab contains a cloud of alcohol vapor. Like jets that leave contrails in the sky, highly energetic particles known as ionizing radiation leave trails when they interact with the evaporated alcohol. Radioactive alpha and beta particles, as well as protons and muons from space, make visible tracks in cloud chambers as they pass though.

Muons are electron-like particles produced when energetic rays from space crash into the molecules in Earth's atmosphere. Muons usually make long, straight tracks. Alpha particles make short, broad tracks and electrons (beta particles) make long, winding paths.

Ruby Payne-Scott b. 1912

SUNSPOTS

A WELL-ROUNDED STUDENT

Ruby Payne-Scott was born in 1912 in New South Wales, a state on the east coast of Australia. As a child, Ruby moved to Sydney to live with her aunt. She attended grade school and high school there, winning honors in both math and biology. At the University of Sydney, she studied physics, chemistry, mathematics, and botany, graduating with a master's degree in physics in 1936.

MAGNETS AND CHICKENS

Ruby worked at a laboratory at the university for a while, studying the effect of strong magnets on developing chicks. She left to teach high school for a few years before eventually landing a job as a librarian at an electronics company that made and operated radios. They discovered her talent for research, and soon Ruby began taking measurements and doing electrical engineering research.

TOP SECRET

During World War II, Ruby joined Australia's Radiophysics Laboratory, where she did top-secret work on radar technology. Before long, Ruby Payne-Scott was Australia's top expert on the radar used to detect enemy aircraft. After the war, she continued to improve radar systems and led the laboratory in a new direction—using radar to examine scientific questions.

NOISY SUNSPOTS

In 1946, the science journal *Nature* published a letter from Ruby showing a correlation between sunspots (bright flares on the sun's surface) and increased electromagnetic radio wave emissions from the sun. She and her colleagues took radio wave measurements from seaside cliff tops that confirmed her theory that sunspots produce radio bursts. Ruby designed a piece of equipment called a swept-lobe interferometer, which scanned the sky, picking up radio signals. This allowed radio astronomers to focus in on certain radio signatures that interested them.

A SECRET WEDDING

Ruby married a man named Bill Hall in 1944, but the wedding was kept secret because married women were not allowed to hold public-service jobs such as hers. When the marriage was discovered, Ruby fought to keep her job. She was fired from her permanent position, although she was permitted to keep working without a job title. When she had children, Ruby was forced to quit work entirely, because there was no maternity leave.

A CAT LOVER

When her son and daughter were older, Ruby Payne-Scott returned to radio astronomy and teaching. Besides science and her family, Ruby loved cats. She also enjoyed walking in the Australian outback and knitting. She died in 1981.

IN TODAY'S WORLD

Ruby's work in radioastronomy helped create the technology used to discover black holes and pulsars. It also helped scientists understand the effect of solar storms on electrical systems on Earth.

SOLAR VIEWER

Project the sun's image onto the end of a shoebox to observe solar events such as eclipses without damaging your vision.

MATERIALS

- 2 shoeboxes or boxes of approximately the same size with lids/flaps removed
- White paper
- Aluminum foil
- Tape
- Pin

Fig. 1. Tape two shoeboxes together.

Fig. 2. Cut a notch on one end and cover it with aluminum foil.

SAFETY TIPS AND HINTS

Do these projects on a clear, sunny day in a spot where the sun is not obscured by trees or houses. Never look at the sun directly or through the pinhole in your box. You could permanently damage your vision. Supervise small children when they are using pins.

Fig. 3. Poke a pinhole in the foil.

Fig. 4. Observe the sun's image.

PROTOCOL

1 Cut and tape the boxes together to make one long box. Cover one interior end with white paper. This will be your solar viewing screen. *Fig. 1.*

2 Cut a large, square notch out of the opposite end of the shoe box and tape aluminum foil over the notch. Keep the foil as tight and smooth as possible. *Fig. 2.*

3 Use a pin to poke a hole slightly larger than the pin itself in the center of the foil. If you make a mistake, replace the foil and try it again. The smaller the hole, the sharper the focus will be. *Fig. 3.*

4 Go outside and stand with the sun directly behind you.

5 Hold the box, opening-side down, with the pinhole pointed at the sun behind you. The foil should be behind you, and the viewing screen should be in front of you. Correct the angle of the box as needed, so that the sun shines through the pinhole and its image is projected on the white paper as a tiny circle. Observe the sun's image. *Fig. 4.*

CREATIVE ENRICHMENT

Save your solar viewing box to use during a solar eclipse.

THE PHYSICS BEHIND THE FUN

When light rays from the sun enter the tiny pinhole, called an aperture, they form an upside-down image of the sun on the paper behind the foil. The image is upside down due to the angle at which the rays of light enter the pinhole and continue to the paper. This allows you to see the sun without looking directly at it.

SUNSPOT VIEWING STATION

Use a pair of binoculars and a tripod to project the sun's image so that the image is large enough to see sunspots.

MATERIALS

- Binoculars
- Tripod
- Duct tape
- White posterboard or trifold foam presentation board

Fig. 1. Attach binoculars to a camera tripod.

Fig. 2. Adjust the angle and focus until you see a double image of the sun.

SAFETY TIPS AND HINTS

Do not look directly at the sun through the binoculars. You could permanently damage your vision.

PROTOCOL

1 Attach binoculars to a camera tripod so the eyepieces are pointing away from the sun and the bigger ends are pointing toward the sun. We used duct tape. The sun should be behind the binoculars. *Fig. 1.*

2 Prop up poster board and adjust the angle of the binoculars on the tripod until double suns (there are two lenses) appear on the white surface.

3 Create a shadow to see the sun's image more clearly. Focus the binoculars. The farther from the binoculars you hold the paper, the larger the image will appear. *Fig. 2 and Fig. 3.*

4 Study the sun's image to look for sunspots—the dark spots on the sun's surface.

Fig. 3. The farther the binoculars are from the paper, the larger the sun's image will appear.

CREATIVE ENRICHMENT

Solar magnetic fields such as the ones that create sunspots can form solar flares that interfere with radio signals. Electromagnetic energy from stoplights can do the same thing to car radios. Next time you are in a car, tune the car's radio to an AM radio station. Listen for radio interference as your car is stopped at stoplights.

THE PHYSICS BEHIND THE FUN

The surface of the sun is a massive sea of churning hot gases. The motion of these electrically conductive gases creates enormous, shifting magnetic fields. Sunspots are visible dark spots on the surface of the sun that form in areas with strong magnetic fields.

When magnetic fields on the sun interact, they can release an explosion of energy called a solar flare, a huge bust of radiation and electromagnetic radio waves, which can interfere with radio signals on Earth. Certain solar flares send a shower of charged particles into Earth's atmosphere. These charged particles are deflected by Earth's magnetic field into spiral paths over the north and south poles, causing visible glowing lights in the sky called aurora borealis or aurora australis (northern and southern lights).

LAB 17

Chien-Shiung Wu b. 1912
SYMMETRY

A SUPPORTIVE FATHER

Born in 1912, Chien-Shiung Wu loved both her parents, but was especially close to her father, who believed that girls should have an education. She and her two brothers grew up in a small fishing village in the Jiangsu province of China. Until she turned eleven and went away to boarding school, Chien attended an elementary school for girls that had been founded by her dad.

A SEA VOYAGE

After graduating at the top of her class, Chien attended National Central University in Nanjing, where she studied math and then physics. She worked in a lab for a few years following graduation and then boarded a ship for America, with plans to attend the University of Michigan for graduate school. After she arrived in San Francisco, a young scientist named Luke Chia-Lu Yuan took her on a tour of the Radiation Laboratory established by Ernest Lawrence in Berkeley.

CHANGE OF PLANS

When Chien heard that women were not allowed to use the front entrance at the University of Michigan, she stayed in Berkeley to pursue her doctoral degree there, in the Radiation Laboratory.

Chien used the cyclotron particle accelerator Dr. Lawrence had developed to study a process called beta decay. To do this, she measured electromagnetic energy, called radiation, which was given off by charged particles when they crashed into other particles. In 1940, Chien received her doctoral degree.

THE MANHATTAN PROJECT

Eventually, Dr. Chien-Shiung Wu married Yuan. Chien and Yuan moved to the east coast, and Dr. Wu taught at Smith College and Princeton, where she was the first woman faculty member of the physics department. During World War II, she joined the Manhattan Project, which was developing the atomic bomb. In addition to improving radiation

detection equipment such as Geiger counters, her expertise solved a problem that was shutting down an important nuclear reactor. After the war, Dr. Wu became a professor at Columbia University in New York.

THE WU EXPERIMENT

As Dr. Wu continued to study beta decay, she was approached by two of her colleagues who were trying to prove a theory they had about how certain subatomic particles behave. They believed certain symmetrical particles that looked identical, but were mirror images of one another, did not always behave in the same way. The men, Dr. Lee and Dr. Yang, had drawn a rough sketch of an experiment out on paper, but didn't have the expertise to perform it themselves.

Dr. Wu developed a technique that allowed her to perform the experiment using strong magnetic fields, extremely low temperatures, and radioactive cobalt. She demonstrated that under the experimental conditions she had created, Lee and Yang's theory was correct. The famous experiment was named the Wu experiment, but her contribution to the groundbreaking work was ignored when Lee and Yang were awarded the 1957 Nobel Prize.

THE WOLF PRIZE

In addition to the Wu experiment, Dr. Wu confirmed Enrico Fermi's theory of beta decay and studied molecular changes in sickle cell disease. She was awarded the prestigious Wolf Prize in 1978. Dr. Wu is buried in her hometown in China in the courtyard of the school her father established.

IN TODAY'S WORLD

Dr. Chien-Shiung Wu was an activist against gender discrimination and is a role model for women in science. She famously said, "I wonder whether the tiny atoms and nuclei, or the mathematical symbols, or the DNA molecules have any preference for masculine or feminine treatment."

MIRROR IMAGES AND SYMMETRY

Use your hands, paint, and paper to learn about objects that may appear to be identical but are not the same.

MATERIALS

- Paper
- Washable paint
- Fruit
- Small notebook (optional)
- Ink pen

SAFETY TIPS AND HINTS

For the autograph book, you'll need plenty of paint or an ink pen that puts out enough wet ink to blot to another page.

PROTOCOL

1 Hold your hands up with the palms facing you and observe them. Now turn them so they face each other. They are mirror images, but they are not identical. Place one hand on top of the other with your palms facing down and you'll see that they are not the same. *Fig. 1 and Fig. 2.*

2 Fold a piece of paper in half. Paint something on one half of the paper and, while the paint is still wet, fold the paper to make a mirror image on the opposite side of the paper. *Fig. 3 and Fig. 4.*

3 When the paper dries, cut each image and try to stack them on top of each other. Like your hands, they are mirror images but are not identical.

Fig. 6. Make a mirror-image autograph page or book.

4 Cut pieces of fruit in half so they are symmetrical. Use the paint to print them on paper. *Fig. 5.*

5 Make a mirror-image autograph book by having people sign one page of a small notebook with plenty of paint or wet ink so their signature extends to the crease between pages. While the ink is still wet, close the book to create a mirror image. Alternatively, use a folded piece of paper. *Fig. 6.*

CREATIVE ENRICHMENT

Look for mirror images in nature and paint what you see. Reflection paintings of lakes and ponds can be accomplished by folding paper in half horizontally and blotting the paint as in step 2 of this project.

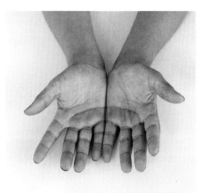

Fig. 1. Human hands are mirror images of one another.

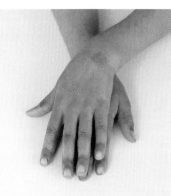

Fig. 2. Although your hands are mirror images of one another, they are not identical.

Fig. 3. Create a painting with reflection symmetry by folding paper to create a central axis.

Fig. 4. Paint on one side of the paper and then fold it to create the mirror image.

Fig. 5. Cut fruit to observe different types of symmetry.

THE PHYSICS BEHIND THE FUN

Symmetry is the quality of being made up of exactly similar parts facing each other or around an axis. There are three main types of symmetry. If something has reflection symmetry, it looks the same on both sides of an imaginary line, like a butterfly does. Objects with rotational symmetry can be spun around a central point and still look the same, like a starfish can. Designs and objects with point symmetry have identical matching parts an equal distance from the same point, but in the opposite direction.

When you cut a piece of fruit in half, you will observe a different type of symmetry depending on whether you divide it from top to bottom or side to side. Although your hands are symmetrical and appear to be identical,

they are mirror images, and if you hold them palm-side down and stack (superimpose) them, you will see they are different.

Chemicals that are mirror images of one another but cannot be superimposed on each other are called chiral. Many chemical structures, called molecules, are chiral and behave differently depending on whether they are "right-handed" or "left-handed." Dr. Chien-Shiung Wu's work demonstrated that like chiral molecules, certain symmetrical subatomic particles that appear to be identical behave differently.

Warren M. Washington b. 1936
ATMOSPHERIC PRESSURE

PORTLAND

Warren M. Washington was born in Portland, Oregon in 1936. He was always interested in science and how things work. Warren's parents had both gone to college and his father worked for the railroad, while his mother worked at home, caring for him and his brother.

A HOMEMADE ALARM CLOCK

When his father brought home a telescope, Warren became fascinated with astronomy. Each time he visited the library, he liked to check out books about famous scientists. He and his brother had a paper route, and together they invented an alarm system using wire and a bell to help their mother wake them up.

CIVIL RIGHTS

At that time, there were very few Black people in Oregon. Warren's family and friends faced frequent racial discrimination. Fortunately, in high school Warren had good teachers who encouraged his interests in both science and social justice. He became involved in the Civil Rights movement, hoping to "contribute to making a change."

SNOWSHOEING

Warren's high school counselor discouraged him from furthering his education, but Warren ignored the bad advice, applied to college, and was accepted to Oregon State University. He earned a bachelor's degree in physics and a master's degree in meteorology—a branch of science concerned with the atmosphere and weather. While he was in graduate school, Warren operated weather radar on a high mountain peak in Oregon and sometimes had to wear snowshoes to hike up to the station.

BOULDER, COLORADO

In 1964, Warren M. Washington became the second African American in history to earn a doctoral degree in meteorology. The first was Charles E. Anderson, who was Warren's mentor. Dr. Washington went to work at the National Center for Atmospheric Research (NCAR) in Boulder, Colorado. He was exceptionally good at his job.

COMPUTER MODELS

Dr. Warren Washington became well known for creating computer models representing the behavior of Earth's atmosphere and climate and predicting the future of Earth's atmosphere. In 1986, Dr. Washington and Dr. Claire Parkinson wrote an important book called *An Introduction to Three-Dimensional Climate Modeling*, which provided information on using data from the atmosphere, the ocean, land/vegetation, and sea ice to understand their relationship with weather and climate.

Dr. Washington is an internationally recognized expert in atmospheric sciences and climate research. He has mentored dozens of students and won a long list of prizes for his pioneering work in meteorology. In addition to mentoring students, Dr. Washington acted as the science advisor for four presidents.

A PRESIDENTIAL HONOR

In 2010, President Barack Obama awarded Dr. Warren M. Washington the National Medal of Science. It is the highest honor that a scientist can receive from the United States government. He also shared in the 2007 Nobel Peace Prize as a member of the Intergovernmental Panel on Climate Change.

IN TODAY'S WORLD

Dr. Warren M. Washington's work has played an essential role in the study of the effects of climate change on our planet.

ATMOSPHERIC PRESSURE

Watch air pressure pop a hard-boiled egg into a bottle as if by magic.

MATERIALS

- A few small or medium-size hard-boiled eggs, shells removed
- Glass bottle, such as a juice bottle, with a neck slightly smaller than a hard-boiled egg
- Birthday candles
- Match or lighter
- Egg cup or small container that will hold an egg upright (optional)

SAFETY TIPS AND HINTS

Because this experiment requires the use of a match or lighter, parental supervision is required. Long hair should be pulled back.

PROTOCOL

1 Set a peeled, hard-boiled egg on the mouth of a glass bottle to verify that it won't easily squeeze through. Remove the egg. *Fig. 1.*

2 Poke two birthday candles into the pointed end of the hard-boiled egg. *Fig. 2.*

3 Hold the egg with the candles pointing up or place it in an egg cup or container to hold it upright.

4 Light the candles and hold the inverted bottle over the candles for a few seconds.

5 Lower the bottle over the candles so it forms a seal on the egg. *Fig. 3.*

Fig. 6. Atmospheric pressure will push the egg into the bottle, where the pressure is lower.

6 Watch the candle go out once it has consumed all the oxygen in the bottle. The pressure inside the bottle will drop, and atmospheric pressure will push the egg up and into the bottle. *Fig. 4 – Fig. 6.*

7 If it does not work the first time, try again. If the egg won't go into the bottle, you may need a slightly smaller egg.

Fig. 1. Try to push a hard-boiled egg into a bottle without breaking it.

Fig. 2. Put two candles in the end of an egg and light them.

Fig. 3. Lower a bottle over the candles so that it forms a seal with the egg.

Fig. 4. When the oxygen in the bottle is used up, the candles will go out.

Fig. 5. You may hear a popping sound as the egg goes into the bottle.

THE PHYSICS BEHIND THE FUN

On Earth, we live in an ocean of air. Air has mass, and gravity gives it weight, so the air above us constantly exerts pressure on us from all directions. Scientists call this phenomenon atmospheric pressure. Atmospheric pressure has an enormous effect on Earth's weather, along with temperature, wind, humidity, precipitation, and cloudiness.

The sun's energy heats the gases in Earth's atmosphere unevenly. Warm air rises, cold air sinks, and the planet rotates, causing area of higher and lower atmospheric pressure. High and low pressure systems push each other around, creating domes and valleys in the atmosphere that rise, swirl, and collide. Atmospheric pressure

controls the formation and movement of thunderstorms, hurricanes, and other weather phenomena, depending on how the weather systems interact with topography (mountains, plains, and valleys) and each other.

This lab uses the force of atmospheric pressure to push an egg into a bottle. Air inside the bottle is heated by a burning candle until the oxygen is used up and the flame goes out. When the candle goes out, the remaining air in the bottle cools rapidly and air pressure drops, creating a partial vacuum. Atmospheric pressure outside the bottle, which is now higher than the pressure inside the bottle, equalizes the pressure by pushing the egg into the bottle.

Stephen Hawking b. 1942
BLACK HOLES

LITTLE "EINSTEIN"

Stephen Hawking was born in Oxford, England in 1942. Both of his parents attended Oxford University, and he had two sisters and an adopted brother. When he was eight, the family moved to St. Albans in Hertfordshire. Their house was big and cluttered, and the entire family read books during meals. Stephen had a group of friends who enjoyed making model airplanes and boats, playing board games, and making homemade fireworks. His math teacher helped Stephen and his friends build a computer out of recycled clocks and electronics.

A TEAM OF FRIENDS

When he was seventeen, Stephen went to school at Oxford University to study physics and mathematics. He was bored and lonely until he joined the rowing team. He went on to graduate school at Cambridge University, where he met Jane Wilde, the woman he would marry.

A CHALLENGE

A year after meeting Jane, Stephen was diagnosed with a disease now called Lou Gehrig's disease, which causes loss of muscle control over time. Although his doctors only gave him two years to live, the disease did not progress as quickly as they thought it would. Stephen married Jane and went back to physics. In 1966, he received his doctoral degree in theoretical physics and applied math. General relativity and cosmology were his specialties.

SINGULARITIES

In 1970, Hawking and the physicist Roger Penrose published a mathematical model showing how the universe could have begun as a singularity, which scientists describe as a breakdown in space and time. He was also interested in cosmic phenomena called black holes. Stephen showed that black holes give off energy, which was named Hawking radiation, and he worked on the problem of what happens to objects when they enter a black hole.

POPULAR SCIENCE

By 1985, Dr. Hawking had used a wheelchair for several years and used a speech-generating device to help him communicate. He wrote a book called *A Brief History of Time*, which explained the complex concepts he studied in a way that everyone could understand. The book sold more than nine million copies. He also wrote several more books, including children's books he wrote with his daughter. Stephen played himself on several popular television shows including *Star Trek*, *The Simpsons*, and *The Big Bang Theory*.

A TRAVELER

Stephen Hawking loved to travel. He dreamed of going to space and got to experience weightlessness on a zero-gravity flight on a jet that did eight parabolic arcs. Dr. Hawking did not, however, believe that time travel is possible. To prove this, he threw a party for time travelers but did not invite anyone, saying that if time travel were possible, people in the future would know about the party and travel back in time to attend it. Nobody showed up.

AN INSPIRATION

Dr. Hawking lived to be seventy-six years old, and his work transformed our understanding of the universe. Although he was very worried about overpopulation and climate change, Stephen Hawking believed that communication is society's most powerful tool, and that communicating will help us to solve the problems facing humanity today and in the future.

IN TODAY'S WORLD

Dr. Stephen Hawking is considered one of the most important physicists of the late twentieth century. His discoveries play an important role in modern cosmology and particle physics.

COLLAPSING STARS & BLACK HOLES

Use playground balls or balloons to learn what happens when stars run out of fuel, shrink, expand, and explode, sometimes collapsing into black holes.

MATERIALS

- Inflatable ball with a valve, such as a beach ball, or ball with a pump and needle
- Balloons

SAFETY TIPS AND HINTS

Do not overinflate balls.

PROTOCOL

1 Squeeze a fully inflated ball to see whether you can make it smaller. Chances are, you cannot, because there is too much pressure in the ball. Like inflated balls, the interiors (inside) of stable stars are under extremely high pressure. *Fig. 1.*

2 While playground balls are filled with pressurized air, the pressure in stars is produced by heat and gases from nuclear reactions that use elements, such as hydrogen, for fuel.

3 To see what happens when a star runs out of fuel and starts to collapse, let some air out of a ball by opening and squeezing the valve or putting a needle in the ball and squeezing it slightly.

4 Close the valve or remove the needle and pretend you are gravity acting on a collapsing ball. Squeeze the ball from all sides, imagining that all the pressure in the ball has been pushed to the center.

Fig. 4. Let all of the air out of the ball.

5 The deflated ball represents a collapsing star. *Fig. 2.*

6 Next, reinflate the ball to its original pressure and imagine the ball expanding until it is much bigger than it is when filled with air.

7 When a star of average mass, like Earth's sun, runs out of its nuclear fuel (hydrogen), the nuclear reactions in the core (center) can no longer produce enough pressure to support the layers of gases above it and the star collapses. During the collapse, the star's core gets smaller, hotter, and denser. These conditions make it possible for some other nuclear fuel to react and give off energy. This stops the collapse of the star. The outer layers expand outwards until the star is more than a hundred times bigger than it was before the center collapsed. This new star is called a red giant. *Fig. 3.*

8 Open the valve or put the needle back into the ball. Let all the air out. Eventually, red giants from sun-size stars will lose most of their mass, leaving behind a trail of star debris, called a nebula, and a small white core called a white dwarf. Supermassive stars are a different story. They go through a similar process at first but form much bigger red giants called red supergiants.

9 Eventually, red supergiants create massive explosions called supernovas and become small, dense neutron stars or black holes. *Fig. 4 and Fig. 5.*

10 To see what happens when a supermassive star runs out of fuel and becomes a black hole, fill a balloon with air. Pop it and squish the rubber down to the smallest ball you can make. Imagine that balloon keeps collapsing toward a single point and keeps collapsing. *Fig. 6 and Fig. 7.*

Fig. 1. Squeeze a fully inflated ball.

Fig. 2. Let some air out of the ball. The slightly deflated ball represents a collapsing star.

Fig. 3. Re-inflate the ball to visualize the formation of a red giant.

Fig. 5. The deflated ball represents a neutron star.

Fig. 6. Pop a balloon to model a supernova.

Fig. 7 Squeeze the balloon into the tiniest ball possible to represent a black hole. Imagine that you could collapse it down to a single point.

CREATIVE ENRICHMENT

Look up the relative sizes of stars, such as Earth's sun, white dwarves, red giants, and super-giants. Use balloons to make models of stars.

THE PHYSICS BEHIND THE FUN

Stars, which are large balls of gases, are always under pressure because gravity is working to collapse them. However, the extremely hot center of a star, called the core, produces enough pressure to keep it from collapsing.

If a star runs out of fuel, the core's temperature drops, the pressure falls, and it collapses. A star the size of our sun will likely start to collapse and then re-expand to become a red giant. More massive stars expand into super giants, which eventually blow up in massive explosions called supernovas. This can give rise to new stars or black holes.

Only stars with twenty times the mass of our sun can become black holes. As a massive star keeps collapsing, the core gets smaller and denser until nothing can escape its gravitational pull. The escape velocity of an object is the speed it must go to escape the gravitational pull of a star. When a massive enough collapsing star is compacted into a small enough sphere, the escape velocity becomes the speed of light. No object can go faster than the speed of light, so nothing inside that sphere can escape from the black hole.

Christine Darden b. 1942

AIRCRAFT WING DESIGN

A TEACHER'S KID

Christine Mann was born in 1920 in Monroe, North Carolina. Her father sold insurance. Christine's mother, a teacher, began bringing Christine to school when she was three years old. By the time she was four, Christine started kindergarten. Soon, she discovered a passion for taking things apart and putting them back together. Breaking down and rebuilding her bike was one of her first projects.

CIVIL RIGHTS

After graduating as the valedictorian of her high school class, Christine attended Hampton University in Virginia. While she was there, she became involved in the early Civil Rights movement and attended some sit-ins with her classmates. She graduated in 1962 with a degree in mathematics, and taught high school for a few years.

AEROSOL PHYSICS

When she was a teacher, Christine married Walter Darden and changed her last name. She got a job in an aerosol physics lab, studying the aerodynamics of how tiny particles move through the air. While working in the lab, she also taught and earned a master's degree in mathematics from Virginia State University.

A HUMAN COMPUTER

In 1967, Christine was hired by NASA to work as one of their "human computers," a group of women who solved mathematical equations for engineers working in the Space Race to safely send humans into space and bring them back to Earth. The Black women working as computers were segregated from the white women with the same jobs. To make doing the calculations more efficient, Christine wrote programs for the early computers at Langley Research Center, where she worked. She and the women she worked with played an integral role in making NASA's first space missions possible.

A GOOD QUESTION

When Christine asked the director at NASA why men were made engineers, while equally qualified women were not given the same opportunity, he was surprised. Nobody had ever asked him the question before. Christine Darden was transferred to the engineering team, earned a Ph.D. in engineering from George Washington University, and was the first African American appointed to the highest rank at Langley Research Center.

SONIC BOOM

In her role as the leader of Langley's Sonic Boom Team, she used computer programs to test aircraft designs. One of Dr. Darden's main jobs was to redesign super-fast aircraft to reduce the shock waves they can cause in the atmosphere. The name *sonic boom* refers to the thunderous sound made by air molecules crashing together when an object moves faster than the speed of sound. She also tested models of airplanes in wind tunnels to study their aerodynamics.

HIDDEN FIGURE

Dr. Christine Darden retired in 2007, but she continues to serve as a role model for young mathematicians, scientists, and engineers. She advises aspiring engineers to picture themselves in their dream job, plan, prepare, and persist. Her story was featured in the film *Hidden Figures*.

IN TODAY'S WORLD

NASA is still working to design supersonic aircraft that produce less noise and environmental impact.

AEROSPACE ENGINEERING

Build a hoop glider and a paper airplane, and then test how well they fly.

MATERIALS

- Ruler
- Scissors
- Printer paper or letter-size (A4) construction paper or card stock
- Tape
- Plastic or biodegradable drinking straw
- Paper clip

SAFETY TIPS AND HINTS

Lightweight paper, such as printer paper, is easier to fold. Heavy paper and card stock last longer and may fly better.

Fig. 9. Test how well your gliders fly.

HOOP GLIDER PROTOCOL

1 Cut one strip of paper about 8½ inches (21 cm) long and 1 inch (2.5 cm) wide and a second strip of paper 5½ inches (14 cm) long and 1 inch (2.5 cm) wide. *Fig. 1.*

2 Tape each strip of paper into a hoop. *Fig. 2.*

3 Use tape to attach the small hoop to one end of the straw. Line the larger hoop up so you can see the smaller hoop through it and tape it to the opposite end of the straw. *Fig. 3.*

4 Throw your glider.

5 Add a paper clip to the small loop so the smaller end of the paper clip goes into the straw if possible.

6 Throw the glider again to see whether it travels farther with the extra weight on the front.

PAPER AIRPLANE PROTOCOL

1 Fold a piece of paper in half the long way to create a crease and then unfold it. *Fig. 4.*

2 Bend the top two corners of paper down to the middle crease and fold them into triangles. *Fig. 5.*

3 Make another fold toward the center like the first, so that the previously folded edges meet at the center crease. *Fig. 6.*

4 Make a third fold, bringing the outside edges to meet in the center crease. *Fig. 7.*

5 Use your fingers and fingernails to smooth and reinforce the folds you made.

6 Pull the last two folds you made apart and bring them down so that they're flat. *Fig. 8.*

7 Grasp the center folds between your thumb and pointer finger and squeeze so the paper airplane is flat on top. Use a paper clip to hold the bottom folds together, if you want to.

8 Throw the paper airplane.

9 Move the paper clip around on the bottom of your plane until you find a position that allows it to fly further. Then, remove the paper clip to see how far it flies. *Fig. 9.*

Fig. 1. Cut two strips of paper, one long and one shorter.

Fig. 2. Tape paper into a hoop.

Fig. 3. Attach the hoops to a straw.

Fig. 4. Fold a piece of paper in half.

Fig. 5. Fold the top corners down to center line.

Fig. 6. Make a second fold to the center.

Fig. 7. Make a third fold.

Fig. 8. Complete the glider.

CREATIVE ENRICHMENT

Make more paper airplanes and hoop gliders. Adjust the designs to optimize how far they will fly.

THE PHYSICS BEHIND THE FUN

Four main forces act on airplanes and gliders. Thrust is the force propelling the aircraft, lift is the upward force, weight is the pull of gravity, and drag is air resistance. Good wing design has an enormous influence on lift and is essential to keeping aircraft aloft.

The study of aerodynamics deals with how air moves around solid objects, and it is essential to airplane design. Air moves more quickly over the curved tops of airplane wings and more slowly over the flat underside. This creates lift by reducing the air pressure on top of the wing.

A hoop glider does not have wings shaped like those on an airplane. However, the curvature of the hoops creates air pressure differences. Your muscles provide thrust for the glider. As you throw it forward, the thin edges of the paper create almost no drag. Air speeds over the top of the hoops and their wide surfaces push down on the air as the air pushes back up, generating lift.

Jocelyn Bell Burnell b. 1943

PULSARS

SPUTNIK

Jocelyn Bell Burnell was born in Lurgan, Northern Ireland in 1923. Her father sparked her interest in the stars by checking out astronomy books from the library and waking Jocelyn and her sister to watch the satellite Sputnik pass. When Jocelyn was thirteen, she went to boarding school in England, where her physics teacher Mr. Tillott encouraged her interest in science.

A BOY'S CLUB

As the only woman studying physics at the University of Glasgow, Jocelyn was harassed by the male students. They whistled, stomped their feet, and banged their desks each time she entered the lecture hall. Jocelyn graduated with honors and a degree in physics, but the experience of feeling so alone stayed with her. From there, she went on to Cambridge University.

A WINDOW TO THE UNIVERSE

Radio physics was a new and exciting field. Bursts of electromagnetic energy from the far reaches of the universe could be detected and recorded as radio signals that made bumps and squiggles on the paper of recording instruments. The farther away objects were, the older they were, so studying far-off objects was like traveling back in time.

SIGNALS FROM SPACE

Jocelyn helped her graduate advisor Anthony Hewish construct a radio telescope that covered four acres and looked like an agricultural frame made of bean poles. While strong signals from deep space registered as strong peaks in the data flowing from the telescope, there were also background radio signals from human activity. Jocelyn was put in charge of running the telescope.

A SQUIGGLE

Every night, Jocelyn went to the university's observatory to analyze signals coming from the radio telescope. She studied 900 feet of paper each day, searching for peaks representing electromagnetic bursts coming from space. One night in 1967, she noticed a funny squiggle on the paper and looked at it more closely to discover something that "shouldn't" happen. Similar peaks appeared on the paper several times at regular intervals, indicating rhythmic pulses of energy from deep space.

Jocelyn contacted Dr. Hewish about her discovery, but he did not believe her until he observed the signal himself and they found it on a second telescope. Soon afterwards, she stumbled uninvited into a meeting in which Dr. Hewish and other men were discussing (without her) the origin of the signal she had discovered.

PULSARS

Later that night, Jocelyn marched back out to the observatory in the freezing cold to point the radio telescope at a different part of the night sky, where she recalled seeing a similar signal. She found it immediately, and the second pulsing signal confirmed that the radio waves were not background noise, but came from an entirely new type of star, which they later called a pulsar.

Dr. Jocelyn Bell Burnell's discovery of pulsars fundamentally changed our understanding of the universe and allowed scientist to test Albert Einstein's (Lab 11) theory of relativity. She was left out, however, when Antony Hewish and Martin Ryle were awarded the 1974 Nobel Prize for Physics. In 2018, she was awarded the Breakthrough Prize and three million dollars, which she donated to the Institute of Physics for a scholarship program to increase diversity in the field.

IN TODAY'S WORLD

Pulsars are important tools for physicists, and they are used to test theories of relativity on a cosmic scale.

PULSARS AND RADIO WAVES

Create pulsar-like radio signal patterns using highlighter pens and build a model of a pulsar using flashlights.

MATERIALS

- Clear tape
- 2 highlighter markers
- White paper, such as printer paper
- Wire hanger (optional)
- Felt-tip markers
- Pencil

SAFETY TIPS AND HINTS

This project works best with two people.

PROTOCOL

1 Use tape to connect two highlighters together with the writing tips facing out. *Fig. 1.*

2 Tape three or more pieces of paper together to make a single, long strip of paper. *Fig. 2.*

3 Place the paper on a flat surface, such as a table, so there is room to pull it from one side of the table to the other.

4 Use a wire hanger with the hooked portion bent up to represent a radio antenna. Set it on the table, away from the paper.

5 Place one marker on the paper and pull the paper from right to left, trying to keep the line centered. Label this line "background radio signals." *Fig. 3.*

Fig. 6. Create a model of a pulsar by using a ball and two flashlights.

6 Replace the paper in its original position.

7 Move the wire hanger "antenna" as if you've pointed it at a different location in space which contains a pulsar.

8 Put one highlighter pen on the spot where the background line begins. The highlighters represent a spinning pulsar sending radio signals picked up by the antenna.

9 Slowly, pull the paper from right to left again, spinning the pens vertically at a constant rate. The lines they make represent radio signals coming from the pulsar. *Fig. 4.*

10 Use a pencil to draw peaks from the line representing background signal to the lines where the highlighter hit the paper, representing stronger radio wave signals. The peaks you see look similar to those seen by Joselyn Bell Burnell when she first encountered a pulsar using her radio antenna. *Fig. 5.*

Fig. 1. Tape two highlighters together, tip-side out.

Fig. 2. Tape several pieces of white paper together to form one long piece of paper.

Fig. 3. Make a line to represent background radio signals.

Fig. 4. Pull the paper from one side to another, spinning the pulsar to make regular marks.

Fig. 5. Use a pencil to draw a line from mark to mark, making a small bump representing a radio signal under each mark.

CREATIVE ENRICHMENT

Look up some illustrations of pulsars and make a 3-D model of a pulsar. For example, you could use a ball and two flash-lights. *Fig. 6.*

THE PHYSICS BEHIND THE FUN

Pulsars are the spinning remains of stars that have exploded at the end of their lives. After going supernova (see Lab 19), what is left of giant stars is astonishingly small (less than ten miles [16 km] across) and very dense. According to Dr. Bell Burnell, "If you jammed the population of the globe into a sewing thimble, it would weigh the same as if it was full of pulsar material."

In this lab, you spin a pair of markers to represent the radio signals of pulsars, which can be picked up as regular, repeating bursts of energy by radio telescopes on Earth. Dr. Bell Burnell says, "Pulsars are visible because they swing a beam of radio waves around the sky, a bit like a lighthouse, and when that beam shines at a radio telescope, you pick up a very accurate pulse, pulse, pulse, pulse—like 'clocks' dotted throughout the galaxy."

Valerie L. Thomas b. 1943
ILLUSION TRANSMITTER

A SELF-STARTER

Valerie L. Thomas was born in Maryland in 1943. She first became interested in science while watching her father fix their television set. Valerie checked a book called *The Boys' First Book of Electronics* out of the library. Although her father refused to help her with the projects in the book, Valerie learned what she could on her own.

PHYSICS CLASS

Valerie's family and most of her teachers were not supportive of her interest in science and engineering, but she took a physics class in school. That class, along with the encouragement of a few teachers, kept her interested in the sciences, and she went to college to study physics at Morgan State University, where she was one of only two women majoring in physics.

NASA

After graduating with a physics degree, Valerie went to work at NASA, analyzing data coming from satellites. She developed computer data systems and oversaw the development of LANDSAT, the longest-running program for collecting satellite data from Earth. Data from these satellites allowed Valerie and her coworkers at NASA to create a system for making predictions about world-wide food crop yields.

ILLUSION TRANSMITTER

An exhibit at a scientific seminar in 1976 caught her attention. Using mirrors, the device gave the illusion that a lightbulb was still glowing, even after it had been turned off. Fascinated, Valerie experimented on her own, using mirrors to produce three-dimensional (3-D) images in front of the glass. In 1977, she used what she'd learned to invent a device called the illusion transmitter. The device, which she patented, was the forerunner of the 3-D technology we use today.

PROBING SPACE

While at NASA, Valerie Thomas became the associate chief of the Space Science Data Operators office. She helped develop technology for NASA's scientific network and the modern internet. Valerie was also involved in projects related to the Voyager Spacecraft, a space probe studying the outer solar system and Halley's Comet.

A ROLE MODEL

Valerie was awarded the Goddard Space Flight Center Award of Merit and NASA's Equal Opportunity Medal. During her career at NASA, and following her retirement in 1995, she made hundreds of school visits, encouraging minorities and women to pursue science and engineering careers.

IN TODAY'S WORLD

Valerie Thomas's ideas are still being used to create modern 3-D technology. The LANDSAT satellite program she created monitors Earth's atmosphere and oceans, tracking climate change. Data coming from these satellites aid the government in everything from land management to helping endangered species.

OPTICAL ILLUSION BOX

Build a glowing optical illusion out of a shoebox, glow sticks, and a mirror.

MATERIALS

- Large shoe box or similar-sized box
- Scissors or a utility knife
- 2 long glow sticks (same color) with connectors (Flat connectors work best.)
- Hot glue
- A dark room
- Makeup (magnifying) mirror on a stand
- Books or boxes to stack

SAFETY TIPS AND HINTS

Small children should be supervised around hot glue and cutting equipment.

PROTOCOL

1 Cut a large opening in one end of the box. If using a shoe box, cut one of the smaller ends. The opening should be big enough that you can position a glow stick made into a circle inside.

Use some of the cardboard to make a viewing hole to attach to the opposite end of the box. Cut a notch approximately 1- x 1-inch (2.5- x 2.5-cm). Use hot glue to attach it to the box.

Activate two glow sticks of the same color. Use connectors to form each of them into a circle.

Hot-glue one connector into the box opening, so that it is inside the box, upside down near the edge. *Fig. 1.*

2 Find a flat surface in a room that can be made dark for the mirror and box. Put a glow stick in the connector inside the box.

Fig. 3. Set the second glow stick on top of the box.

3 Put your eye to the eye hole of the viewing box. Hold the box in front of the magnifying mirror so that you can see the glow stick. *Fig. 2.*

4 Slowly back away from the mirror until you pass the focal point and the image flips over, so that the glow stick appears to be on top of the box.

5 Set the box on books or other boxes so that when you look through the viewing hole, you only see the glow stick. You can play with the angle of the mirror.

6 Set the other glow stick on top of the box above the upside-down glow stick. *Fig. 3.*

7 Look through the eye hole and readjust as needed, so you only see the glow stick on the box and the reflection of the glow stick in the box. *Fig. 4.*

8 Turn the lights off. While looking through the eye hole, remove the glow stick on top of the box. The reflection of the glow stick in the box will remain, but it will appear that it is on top of the box. *Fig. 5 – Fig. 7.*

Perform this trick for a friend or family member who doesn't know that there's a second glow stick inside the box.

CREATIVE ENRICHMENT

Use a makeup mirror to flip the image of a lighted lightbulb on the wall behind it. Build a more complicate version of an illusion box using lightbulbs or LEDs.

Fig. 1. Hot-glue a glow-stick connector onto the bottom of a hole in a shoe box.

Fig. 2. Use a magnifying mirror to flip the image of the glow stick in the box so that it appears to be on top of the box.

Fig. 4. Look through the eyehole and adjust so that you see only the glowstick on top and a reflection in the mirror.

Fig. 5. Turn the lights off.

Fig. 6. While looking through the hole, removed the glowstick on top.

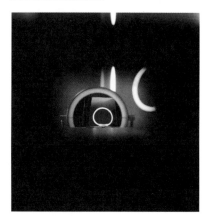

Fig. 7. The reflection will remain, as if the glow stick were still there.

THE PHYSICS BEHIND THE FUN

Light rays are reflected off shiny surfaces at the same angle that they encounter them. When an object is placed a certain distance from a concave (curved inwards) magnifying mirror, light coming from an object can be reflected so the image appears to be the same size but is inverted (upside down) in the mirror.

In this lab, when you line the glow stick on top of the box up with the glow stick inside the box, it appears to the observer that they are looking at a single glow stick. When you remove the glow stick on the box, they are left looking at the flipped image of the upside-down glow stick hidden in the box.

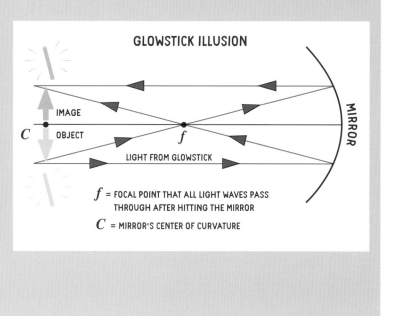

GLOWSTICK ILLUSION

f = FOCAL POINT THAT ALL LIGHT WAVES PASS THROUGH AFTER HITTING THE MIRROR

C = MIRROR'S CENTER OF CURVATURE

Nadya Mason b. 1972
CONDUCTIVITY/CARBON

POKING AT ANT HILLS

From the time she was young, Nadya Mason has been interested in the world around her. As a child, she loved nature and satisfied her curiosity by running around picking fruit from trees and poking at anthills with sticks. Born in New York City, she lived in Brooklyn until she was six. Her family then moved to Washington D.C. and later to Houston, Texas, so she got to experience life in several cities as she was growing up.

A WORLD-CLASS GYMNAST

An exceptionally talented athlete, Nadya ran track and was a gymnast on the United States National team. In addition to sports, she was an excellent student who became interested in math at a young age. It wasn't until she had an opportunity to work in a biochemistry lab that she discovered her love of hands-on science and realized for the first time that it was possible to make science her career.

ATOMIC AMBITIONS

After high school, she went to Harvard University, where she took as many science and math classes as she could. Soon Nadya discovered that she likes physics the best. The science of atoms, the building blocks of matter, described the world in a way she understood and connected with. Her parents were supportive of the idea that Nadya would be a physicist and encouraged her to pursue her dreams.

A PROFESSOR

After getting her bachelor's degree at Harvard, she continued her studies at Stanford University, where she received her doctoral degree. Dr. Nadya Mason, returned to Harvard to do some post-doctoral research before becoming an assistant professor and then a full professor at the University of Illinois Urbana-Champaign. Besides doing research there, she loves working with her students.

ELECTRON INTERACTIONS

Dr. Mason's laboratory focuses on how charged particles called electrons move through different materials, how they interact with each other, and why they conduct electricity the way that they do. She's especially interested in how electrons behave in very thin layers or small quantities of different materials. She has worked extensively with carbon, graphene, and other materials whose properties she studies. Nadya explains, "we work with carbon nanotubes that are just one-billionth of a meter in diameter but up to centimeters long; think of them as the tiniest wires you can make."

HANDS-ON THINKING

In addition to being an exceptional scientist, Dr. Mason is passionate about diversity issues that affect the scientific community. She works hard as a science communicator to encourage everyone to follow their interests in science, rather than being intimated it. Dr. Mason gave a TED talk in 2019 titled "How to spark your creativity, scientifically," in which she reminded her audience that "hands-on thinking (through experimentation) connects our understanding and even our vitality to the physical world and the things that we use." She has won several awards, including the American Physical Society's Maria-Goeppert Mayer Award and was a general counselor to the American Physical Society (APS) and chair of the APS Committee on Minorities.

IN TODAY'S WORLD

Dr. Mason's research on electron movement through very small quantities of material could have an enormous impact on modern technology. She concludes her earlier statement on carbon nanotubes, "What sort of electronic behavior can you expect from something only a few atoms across? Is it just what you'd expect from a bigger wire—or does something different happen? The answer is that something different happens . . . which, I would think, would be very relevant to the computer industry which has a stake in making computers keep working no matter how small they get."

GRAPHITE CIRCUIT

Draw a graphite path for electrons that carries enough electricity to light an LED.

MATERIALS

- Paper
- Graphite pencil or crayon (A No.2 pencil works well for the enrichment activity, but a softer lead such as a #9B graphite crayon is best for graphite circuits.)
- 2 alligator clip test leads
- 9-volt battery
- Several small LEDs
- Scotch tape (optional)
- Camera, such as one on a phone

SAFETY TIPS AND HINTS

Adult supervision recommended. The battery can get hot. Unhook all test leads from the battery when you are finished using them.

Fig. 4. Move the LED wire closer to the alligator clip to see what happens, but don't touch it.

PROTOCOL

1 On a piece of printer paper, use a graphite pencil or crayon to draw a thick, black line, about 1¾ inches (4 cm) long and ½ (1 cm) wide. Color over it again and again until you create a solid layer of graphite on the paper containing no spaces or gaps. *Fig. 1.*

2 Hook each of the two wires up to the battery so that one is connected to each terminal.

3 Clip the wire attached to the positive battery terminal to one wire of an LED bulb. *Fig. 2.*

4 Touch the free wire of the LED bulb to one end of the line you drew. *Fig. 3.*

5 Touch the alligator clip attached to the negative battery terminal to the opposite end of the graphite line. *Fig. 3.*

6 Move the LED wire closer to the alligator clip to see what happens. It should get brighter as you decrease the distance. Try not to touch the bulb directly to the clip. *Fig. 4.*

7 If the bulb doesn't light up, switch the positive alligator clip to the other wire of the LED bulb and try it again. If it still doesn't work, make sure there are no gaps in the line you drew and try a different LED.

8 Create some new drawing with the graphite pencil or crayon to see whether the electrical current follows the graphite around corners and curves. What happens if you erase part of the line to create a gap? *Fig. 5 and Fig. 6.*

Fig. 1. Use soft graphite to draw a heavy line.

Fig. 2. Connect alligator test leads to each battery terminal and one LED terminal.

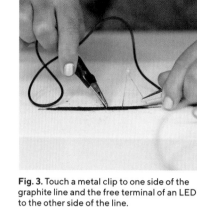

Fig. 3. Touch a metal clip to one side of the graphite line and the free terminal of an LED to the other side of the line.

Fig. 5. Erase part of the line and test whether the electrical current can still light the bulb when the carbon layer has been disrupted.

Fig. 6. Can electrons jump the gap, or do you need a layer of graphite to act as a path (conductor) for electrons?

Fig. 7. Use pencil and tape to make ultra-thin layers of graphite.

CREATIVE ENRICHMENT

Make ultra-thin layers of graphite by lifting it onto tape. Use a pencil to scribble a solid rectangle around 1¾ inches (4 cm) long and about 1 inch (2 cm) wide. Use a piece of tape to lift the carbon from the paper. Use a second piece of tape to carefully lift carbon from the first. Repeat with more pieces of tape until you can't lift any more carbon, placing the pieces of tape under the original rectangle. Take a photo of the tape and observe how the graphite flake size changes.

THE PHYSICS BEHIND THE FUN

If you've ever been shocked by a doorknob, you know from experience that some metals are excellent conductors of electricity. Conductors are substances that electrical current, which is similar to a river of charged particles called electrons, can flow through easily. Copper, silver, aluminum, gold, brass, and steel are all good conductors.

Graphite is a crystalline form of carbon and is often used to make pencil lead. In addition to marking paper, graphite is a good conductor of electricity and can be used to create a circuit, which is a path for electrical current. In this experiment, when you draw a solid graphite line on paper, the thin layer of graphite that you lay down carries enough electrical charge to light a bulb.

Chanda Prescod-Weinstein b. 1982
COSMOLOGY

A BASEBALL FAN

Chanda Prescod-Weinstein was born in the El Sereno neighborhood of Los Angeles, California, where the Tongva village of Otsungna stood until Spanish colonizers arrived around 1770. El Sereno is near Dodger Stadium, and as a kid Chanda became a huge fan of the Dodgers baseball team. In addition to dreaming of becoming a professional baseball player, she played piano, flute, and saxophone.

READING, DANCING, AND MATH

When she was young, Chanda loved practicing her multiplication tables. Soon, she became comfortable with mathematics, which is the language of physics. In high school, books such as Stephen Hawking's *A Brief History of Time* got her excited about black holes and the building blocks of the universe. In addition to reading and studying, Chanda attended a performing arts school, where she trained as a dancer in both modern dance and jazz.

FRESHMAN PHYSICS

Chanda attended Harvard University, where she earned degrees in physics and astronomy. Despite finding her freshman physics class somewhat boring, she later realized that the simple experiments they did in class built a solid foundation that would help her solve more interesting and complicated problems in the future.

A MENTOR

Most of Chanda's physics professors and classmates were white men, so she had to create her own vision of herself as a physicist. When she was almost done with her undergraduate degree, she finally met a Black woman with a doctoral degree in physics—Dr. Nadya Mason (Lab 23), who became a role model and a mentor. Chanda got a master's degree in astronomy, a doctoral degree in theoretical physics, and a job as an assistant professor in physics and core faculty in women's and gender studies at the University of New Hampshire.

UNIVERSAL QUESTIONS

As a theoretical physicist, Dr. Chanda Prescod-Weinstein uses math to solve the mysteries of the universe. She has a unique viewpoint because she "sits on the fence" between the disciplines of astronomy and physics, which ask similar questions in different ways. Scientists think that the universe contains a lot of invisible stuff, called dark energy and dark matter, along with "a tiny smidgeon of everyday stuff like us." Dr. Prescod-Weinstein uses ideas from physics and astronomy to learn more about dark matter and address questions about how everything in the universe "got to the be the way it is."

AN AUTHOR AND AN ACTIVIST

Besides studying particles physics, Dr. Prescod-Weinstein is a popular science communicator and an activist for equality in science. She is a Pilates instructor, loves *Star Trek*, and does research on feminist science studies. Chanda believes that everyone should have the chance to see the dark night sky and an opportunity to learn about the universe. Her book *The Disordered Cosmos: A Journey into Dark Matter, Spacetime, and Dreams Deferred* explores these ideas. A well-respected scientist, she has received several prestigious awards for her work in particle physics, astrophysics, and astronomy.

IN TODAY'S WORLD

Scientists are currently using data collected by ground-based and space observatories to study the light coming from 35 million galaxies. They hope to reconstruct how the universe has been expanding over the last 11 billion years. Ideally, this work will help us understand the nature of dark energy.

EXPANDING UNIVERSE MODEL

Make Cosmic Pizza Dough to visualize how the universe is expanding.

MATERIALS

- 2 teaspoons (8 g) yeast (or 1 teaspoon [4 g] if you like flatter crust)
- 1 cup (235 ml) warm water (not hot)
- 3 cups (375 g) all-purpose flour
- 1 teaspoon (6 g) salt
- 1 tablespoon (15 ml) olive oil
- Oregano, poppy seeds, or another small, edible ingredient to add to the pizza dough
- Pizza toppings (optional)
- Large bowl
- Greased baking sheet, pizza stone, or pizza-size grilling basket
- Balloon (optional)
- Permanent marker (optional)
- Food coloring (optional)
- Toothpicks (optional)

Fig. 6. Enjoy your cosmic pizza.

SAFETY TIPS AND HINTS

An adult should supervise oven use.

PROTOCOL

1 Add the yeast to the warm water. Let it sit for 5 minutes. Yeast is a living organism that produces carbon dioxide gas as it eats carbohydrates, such as flour and sugar.

2 In a large bowl, mix the flour with the salt and 1 tablespoon of the spices or seeds you chose to represent cosmic objects, such as galaxies. *Fig. 1.*

3 Stir 1 tablespoon (15 ml) of olive oil and yeast mixture into the flour mixture.

4 Briefly knead the dough and then put it back in the bowl and cover it with plastic wrap or a damp dish towel. Optional: Use a toothpick to make small pairs of food coloring marks in the dough, representing stars. Measure and record the distance between them so that you can re-measure them when the dough has expanded to see how far they have moved away from each other. *Fig. 2 and Fig. 3.*

5 Let the dough rise for 1 hour or so. *Fig. 4.*

6 Observe how the poppy seeds or spices spread out, moving away from each other in all directions as gas produced by the yeast makes the dough expand. The rising dough is a simple model of our expanding universe.

7 Preheat an oven to 400°F (205°C). Punch the dough down. Coat it with extra flour, if needed, so it is not too sticky. Stretch or toss your pizza dough, add toppings, and bake the pizza an oven or on a grill for around 20 minutes or until the cheese is golden-brown. Turn on the oven light as your pizza bakes to watch the crust puff up even more. Enjoy eating your cosmic pizza! *Fig. 5 and Fig. 6.*

Fig. 1. Mix dough, including seeds or spices to represent cosmic objects.

Fig. 2. Knead the dough and put it in a bowl.

Fig. 3. Mark the dough with dots of food coloring to measure expansion.

Fig. 4. Let the dough rise for an hour or two. Measure expansion.

Fig. 5. Stretch the dough.

Fig. 7. Pinch a balloon to imagine how curved space might form a wormhole.

CREATIVE ENRICHMENT

Draw dots representing stars or galaxies on a balloon and blow it up. Pinch the balloon to see how two points an enormous distance apart could come together if space is distorted. *Fig. 7.*

Scientists wonder whether space could curve to form areas called wormholes, where space is pinched together by objects such as black holes. Science fiction writers dream of traveling through wormholes to move between objects millions of light years apart quickly.

THE PHYSICS BEHIND THE FUN

Only the tiniest fragment of the universe is made up of everyday, visible matter, like you and me. Most of the universe is empty space. When looking at certain objects in the universe, scientists noticed that things do not add up as expected. Dark matter, first described by the physicist Vera Rubin, is the name given to a mysterious substance that could account for many of the observations that physicists do not understand. Some physicists and astronomers, such as Dr. Prescod-Weinstein, believe that certain "super symmetric" particles may be candidates for dark matter.

From studying stars and other cosmic objects, scientists have concluded the universe is expanding. In this lab, you use rising bread dough to model the expansion of the universe outwards in all directions, while poppy seeds or spices represent galaxies and other cosmic objects moving away from each other as the universe spreads out.

≡ LAB 25 ≡
Burçin Mutlu-Pakdil b. 1986
GALAXIES

ISTANBUL

Burçin Mutlu-Pakdil was born in the Turkish city of Istanbul, which lies in both Europe and Asia. Istanbul is an ancient, famous city that went by the names Byzantium and Constantinople in the past. Burçin's grandparents never learned to read or write and her parents, who were born and raised in a small town, were not able to pursue an education beyond the fifth grade due to financial issues. Despite those challenges, her parents believed strongly in education.

REACHING FOR THE STARS

In middle school, Burçin became interested in physics when she read a book about Albert Einstein. She had always liked looking at the stars, and now she wanted to learn more about them. Her family encouraged her to go away to college to study physics, and despite the disapproval of some friends and relatives, Burçin left Istanbul to attend Bilkent University in Ankara, Turkey.

FOCUSING ON PHYSICS

When Burçin arrived at college, one of her male professors told her it was crazy for a woman to leave her hometown to study physics. At the university, she was not allowed to wear her hijab and constantly battled prejudice while she pursued her degree. Despite all the obstacles, she refused to let anything stand in her way, and remained focused on her passion until she graduated. Burçin then moved to the United States to study astrophysics, earning a master's degree from Texas Tech and a Ph.D. from the University of Minnesota. Today, Dr. Burçin Mutlu-Pakdil studies the most mysterious objects in the universe at the University of Chicago.

BURÇIN'S GALAXY

Burçin and her research team first spotted a very peculiar object in the background while studying another galaxy. At first glance, it is a beautiful celestial object that has a ball of yellowish stars surrounded by a single ring of blue stars, with nothing visible connecting the two. Galaxies like these are extremely rare. When looking at the galaxy in different lights, they unexpectedly discovered an additional unique structure—a second inner ring, making this galaxy the first example of an elliptical galaxy with two symmetric rings. This unique, beautiful elliptical galaxy, 359 million light years away, is now commonly called Burçin's Galaxy.

UNIVERSAL MYSTERIES

Dr. Burçin Mutlu-Pakdil uses some of the largest telescopes in the world. She travels to locations such as Hawaii and Chile to collect data and study scientific mysteries, such as dark matter and how the faintest and smallest galaxies form and evolve in the universe. In addition to having a galaxy named after her, she has won many awards for her work in physics and is a role model for young scientists. She says, "I do not want to blend in, I want to stand out as stars do, so I fought against all these stereotypes and worked hard to live beyond the labels."

IN TODAY'S WORLD

Our galaxy, the Milky Way, formed around 14 billion years ago, attracting heavy elements that came together to form the sun, our planet, and everything on it. Using powerful tools such as the Keck telescopes in Hawaii, astronomers can see the light from 100 billion other galaxies. Each of these galaxies contains 100 billion stars. By using spectra (See Lab 13) collected by the telescopes, astronomers are discovering what the galaxies are made of. They hope to learn more about the universe and whether there may be other galaxies containing planets that could support life.

COSMIC ART

Use food coloring and corn syrup or gelatin to create images of galaxies and other cosmic objects.

MATERIALS

- Corn syrup
- Small white bowls or white plates with flat bottoms
- Food coloring
- Toothpicks, skewers, or sharp pencils
- Food-decorating sprinkles (optional)
- Plain gelatin (optional)
- Flat plastic lids (optional)
- Flashlight (optional)

SAFETY TIPS AND HINTS

Throw the orbiting galaxies outdoors. Use caution with hot gelatin.

PROTOCOL

1 Look up photographs of Burçin's galaxy and other galaxies, supernovas, nebulas, and black holes.

2 Pour a thin layer of corn syrup into the bottom of a small flat bowl or plate.

3 Choose one of the cosmic images you found to duplicate using food coloring. The colors do not have to match.

4 Drip food coloring onto the corn syrup. Use a toothpick tip to swirl the colors into the design. Add sprinkles, if you want, to represent planets and interstellar dust. It may take some practice.

5 When you create a cool cosmic design, take a picture of it. *Fig. 1 and Fig. 2.*

Fig. 1. Use food coloring and a toothpick to create galaxies in corn syrup.

Fig. 2. Add sprinkles to represent cosmic objects.

CREATIVE ENRICHMENT

Instead of corn syrup, use melted gelatin to make galaxy art on lighting gels. Melt ½ ounce plain gelatin in 1 cup (235 ml) of water, cool for 10 minutes, and pour into the clear flat lids of recyclable containers. Use food coloring to make designs and allow the gels to solidify and dry. Remove the gels from the plastic lids. Shine a flashlight through the designs to project cosmic images on a wall or piece of paper. *Fig. 5 – Fig. 8.*

Use sunlight to project the image you made.

Fig. 5. Create galaxies in gelatin on plastic lids.

Fig. 6. Let them solidify and dry.

Fig. 7. Remove dried gelatin from the lids.

Fig. 8. A flashlight also works well to project the image from your gelatin design.

Try projecting your images in a dark room.

ORBITING GALAXY

Use balls on a string to test how galaxies connected by gravity might move together through space.

MATERIALS

- Rope, twine, cord, or yarn
- Perforated balls, such as Wiffle balls (large, small, or both)
- Duct tape

PROTOCOL

1 Cut a piece of rope, twine, cord, or yarn about 3 feet (1 m) long.

2 Thread it through a Wiffle ball and tie it to attach the ball to one end of the cord.

3 Repeat with a second ball, so you have a ball tied to each end. Each ball will represent a galaxy.

4 When using small balls, cover them with several layers of duct tape to make them heavier. *Fig. 1.*

5 If you have both large and small balls, make a second rope with a large ball on one end and a small ball on the other. *Fig. 2.*

6 Make another set of connected galaxies using a shorter piece of rope.

Fig. 4. Throw them to see how they rotate through space.

7 Take the galaxy ropes outdoors to an open space. Holding them by one end, throw them to see how two galaxies connected by gravity stay together, even as they move through space. Compare how they rotate and move, depending on "galaxy" size and the distance between them. *Fig. 3 and Fig. 4.*

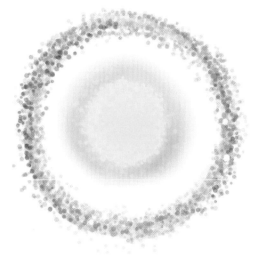

Fig. 1. Attach balls to strings and use duct tape to make them heavier.

Fig. 2. Use different-size balls and various string lengths.

Fig. 3. Compare two connected galaxies at a time.

THE PHYSICS BEHIND THE FUN

A galaxy is a beautiful collection of stars and the remains of stars, interstellar dust, gases, and dark matter, all bound together by gravity. Many are thought to have massive black holes at their center. In the vast expanse of space, galaxies are not alone, but are connected to one or more other galaxies by a web of gravity.

Astronomers organize galaxies by shape. They can be elliptical (spherical or egg-shaped), spiral, or irregular. Along with the Andromeda Galaxy, our galaxy, the Milky Way, is part of a group of galaxies called the Local Group inside of the Virgo Supercluster. Each galaxy has specific motions within itself and in relationship to other galaxies. The Milky Way is so big that it has at least sixty smaller satellite galaxies orbiting it.

In this lab, you can explore the shapes of different galaxies and see how two galaxies connected by gravity might move through space, like balls on either end of a rope.

Glossary

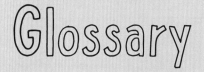

Atmospheric Pressure: We live under an ocean of air. The air's pressure is exerted in every direction at any given point by the weight of the atmosphere. On Earth's surface, atmospheric pressure affects weather, temperature, wind, humidity, precipitation, and clouds due to pressure differences between warm and cold air.

Beta Decay: Beta decay is a radioactive transformation (change) that happens in the nucleus of an atom when an unstable element ejects or captures a beta particle. Beta particles are high-energy, charged subatomic particles called electrons and positrons.

Black Hole: A black hole is a celestial body with a gravitational field so strong that even light cannot escape it. Black holes are created when massive stars collapse. There is a supermassive black hole at the center of the Milky Way galaxy called Sagittarius A.

Chiral: Chiral molecules are members of a pair of chemicals that are mirror images of each other but cannot be superimposed (stacked) on each other.

Conductors: Conductors are substances that can transmit (carry) electricity and heat. Electrical current can flow easily through conductors such as copper, silver, aluminum, gold, brass, and steel.

Cosmology: A branch of astronomy dealing with the origin, structure, development, and space-time relationships of the universe.

Cyclotron: A machine also called a particle accelerator that uses magnets and electricity to create a beam of fast-moving charged particles that speed along a spiral pathway to create a beam. The beam of charged particles is crashed into other particles to study the structure of the nucleus of atoms. Cyclotrons are also used to create radioactive elements for medical use.

Dark Energy and Dark Matter: Dark energy is a hypothetical, undetectable form of energy that is believed to cause the accelerating expansion of the universe. Scientists believe that dark matter exists because visible (known) matter cannot account for certain gravitational effects they observe when studying objects in the universe.

Electron: A stable subatomic particle carrying a negative charge. Electrons are found in all atoms and carry electricity in conductive material.

Fission: The nucleus is the center of an atom. Fission is the splitting of an atomic nucleus into approximately equal parts. When elements such as uranium and plutonium are split, enormous quantities of energy are released.

General Theory of Relativity: A theory by which Albert Einstein explored the relationship between space, time, and gravity.

Illusion Transmitter: A device using parabolic (curved) mirrors to produce three-dimensional (3-D) images. It is used by NASA and was the forerunner of the modern medical imaging and 3-D technology we use today.

Neutron: An uncharged subatomic particle with a mass nearly equal to that of the proton. It is unstable by itself but can be stabilized when joined to a proton. Neutrons are found in all known atomic nuclei (the centers of atoms) except for hydrogen.

Piezoelectricity: Electricity created by distorting (squeezing or stretching) a crystal such as quartz.

Proton: A subatomic particle that is a part of all atomic nuclei (the centers of atoms). Protons carry a positive charge that is numerically equal to the negative charge of an electron.

Pulsar: A celestial source of pulsating electromagnetic radiation (radio waves). There is a short and relatively constant interval between pulses.

Radiation: The process of sending out energy in the form of subatomic particles and/or waves. Some radioactive substances, such as dust containing radioactive elements, radon gas, and ultraviolet light from the sun, can be harmful to humans.

Red Giant: Some red giants are formed from sun-sized stars when they run out of fuel and collapse under their own weight. Supermassive stars form red supergiants that create massive explosions called supernovas and become neutron stars or black holes.

Sonic Boom: A sonic boom is the sound of shock waves created when an object travels through the air faster than the speed of sound. The explosive sound is often produced when a shock wave formed at the nose of a supersonic aircraft reaches the ground.

Spectroscopy: A technique that uses a prism or a light-splitting structure called a diffraction grating to split light waves from an object, such as a star, into its different wavelengths. It is a powerful tool used by astronomers to study stars and learn what elements they contain.

Spectrum: Every celestial object has a light signature called a spectrum. Physicists use a device called a spectrometer to analyze light coming into a telescope from a single area or object, such as a star.

Swept-Lobe Interferometer: A device used by astronomers to scan the sky and pick up radio signals.

Symmetry: Something with *reflection symmetry* looks the same on both sides of an imaginary line. An object with *rotational symmetry* can be spun around a central point and still look the same. *Point symmetry* means an object's parts are identical and are an equal distance from the same point, but in the opposite direction.

Wormholes: Scientists predicted that a black hole's surface might (in theory) work as a bridge connecting to a second patch of space. This hypothetical structure of space-time referred to as a wormhole is described as a tunnel connecting points separated in space and time.

References and Resources

LAB 2

Cowell, Alan. "Vatican Says Galileo Was Right: It Moves." *New York Times,* October 31, 1992. nytimes. com/1992/10/31/world/after-350-years-vatican-says-galileo-was-right-it-moves.html

History.com "Galileo Galilei." October 24, 2019. history.com/topics/inventions/galileo-galilei

LAB 3

NASA. "About the Hubble Space Telescope." hubblesite.org/mission-and-telescope/the-telescope

Ravilious, Kate. "Isaac Newton: Who He Was, Why Apples Are Falling." *National Geographic,* March 12, 2020. nationalgeographic.org/article/isaac-newton-who-he-was-why-apples-are-falling/7th-grade

Smith, George. "Isaac Newton." *The Stanford Encyclopedia of Philosophy* (Fall 2008 Edition), Edward N. Zalta (ed.) plato.stanford.edu/archives/fall2008/entries/newton

Wikipedia contributors. "Isaac Newton." *Wikipedia, The Free Encyclopedia.* en.wikipedia. org/w/index.php?title=Isaac_Newton&oldid=1027240452 (accessed June 7, 2021).

LAB 5

King, Allen L. "Count Rumford, Sanborn Brown, and the Rumford Mosaic." *Dartmouth College Library Bulletin.* dartmouth.edu/library/Library_Bulletin/Apr1995/King_Rumford.html

LAB 6

American Physical Society. "May 1801: Thomas Young and the Nature of Light." *APS News.* (May 2008; Volume 17, number 5). aps.org/publications/apsnews/200805/physicshistory.cfm

Swinburne University of Technology. "Spectroscopy." astronomy.swin.edu. au/cosmos/S/Spectroscopy

LAB 7

American Physical Society. "July 1816: Fresnel's Evidence for the Wave Theory of Light." *APS News.* (July 2016; Volume 25, number 7). aps.org/publications/apsnews/201607/physicshistory.cfm

LAB 8

The Royal Institution. "Michael Faraday (1791-1867): Biography of Michael Faraday." rigb.org/our-history/people/f/michael-faraday

LAB 9

American Physical Society. "March 1880: The Curie Brothers Discover Piezoelectricity." *APS News.* (March 2014; Volume 23, number 3). aps.org/publications/apsnews/201607/physicshistory.cfmaps.org/publications/apsnews/201403/physicshistory.cfm

Locke, Susannah. "Why Do Wintergreen Candies Spark in The Dark?" *Scienceline,* May 19, 2008. scienceline.org/2008/05/ask-locke-lifesavers

LAB 10

Conkling, Winifred. *Radioactive!: How Irène Curie and Lise Meitner Revolutionized Science and Changed the World.* Algonquin Books, 2016.

Wikipedia contributors. "Lise Meitner." *Wikipedia, The Free Encyclopedia.* en.wikipedia. org/w/index.php?title=Lise_Meitner&oldid=1027280436 (accessed June 7, 2021).

LAB 11

The Nobel Prize. "Albert Einstein: Biographical." nobelprize.org/prizes/physics/1921/einstein/biographical/

Clark, Stuart. "Why Einstein Never Received a Nobel Prize for Relativity." *The Guardian.* October 8, 2012. theguardian.com/science/across-the-universe/2012/oct/08/einstein-nobel-prize-relativity

Wikipedia contributors. "Albert Einstein." *Wikipedia, The Free Encyclopedia.* en.wikipedia. org/w/index.php?title=Albert_Einstein&oldid=1027249539 (accessed June 7, 2021).

LAB 12

National Inventors Hall of Fame. "Katharine Burr Blodgett." invent.org/inductees/katharine-burr-blodgett

Owles, Eric. "G.E.'s History of Innovation." *The New York Times,* June 12, 2017. nytimes.com/2017/06/12/business/general-electric-history-of-innovation.html

Whelan, M. and Dr. Edwin Reilly, Jr. "Katharine Burr Blodgett: Pioneer in Surface Chemistry and Engineering." Edison Tech Center. edisontechcenter. org/Blodgett.html

Wikipedia contributors. "Katharine Burr Blodgett." *Wikipedia, The Free Encyclopedia.* en.wikipedia.org/w/index.php?title=Katharine_Burr_Blodgett&oldid=995216375 (accessed June 7, 2021).

LAB 13

American Physical Society. "January 1, 1925: Cecilia Payne-Gaposchkin and the Day the Universe Changed." *APS News.* (January 2015; Volume 24, number 1). ahttps://www.aps.org/publications/apsnews/201501/physicshistory.cfmps.org/publications/apsnews/201501/physicshistory.cfm

Crockett, Christopher. "Cecilia Payne-Gaposchkin Revealed Stars' Composition and Broke Gender Barriers." *ScienceNews.* March 1, 2020. sciencenews.org/article/cecilia-payne-gaposchkin-revealed-stars-composition-broke-gender-barriers

Fabbiano, Giuseppina. "The Woman Who Explained the Stars." *Nature.* February 24, 2020. nature.com/articles/d41586-020-00509-3

NASA. "Spectroscopy: Reading the Rainbow." hubblesite.org/contents/articles/spectroscopy-reading-the-rainbow

Wikipedia contributors. "Cecilia Payne-Gaposchkin." *Wikipedia, The Free Encyclopedia.* en.wikipedia.org/w/index.php?title=Cecilia_Payne-Gaposchkin&oldid=1025476326 (accessed June 7, 2021). https://en.wikipedia.org/wiki/Cecilia_Payne-Gaposchkin

LAB 14

Blakemore, Erin. "Google Doodle Honors Little-Known Math Genius Who Helped America Reach the Stars." *Smithsonian Magazine."* March 29, 2017. smithsonianmag.com/smithsonian-institution/little-known-math-genius-helped-america-reach-stars-180962700

Viola, Herman. "Mary Golda Ross: She Reached for the Stars." *American Indian.* (Volume 19, Number 4). americanindianmagazine.org/story/mary-golda-ross-she-reached-stars

LAB 15

BU News Service. "Muon Tomography and Its Ability to Probe the Unseeable." March 20, 2019. bunewsservice.com/muon-tomography-and-its-ability-to-probe-the-unseeable/

Woithe, Julia. *Cloud Chamber. S'Cool LAB -Do-It-Yourself Manual.* Version 7. scoollab.web.cern.ch/sites/scoollab.web.cern.ch/files/documents/20200521_JW_DIYManual_CloudChamber_v7.pdf

Zych, Ariel. "Build a Cloud Chamber." *Science Friday.* October 16, 2015. sciencefriday.com/educational-resources/build-a-cloud-chamber/

LAB 16

Wikipedia contributors. "Ruby Payne-Scott." Wikipedia, The Free Encyclopedia. en.wikipedia.org/w/index.php?title=Ruby_Payne-Scott&oldid=1025023042 (accessed June 7, 2021).

"Overlooked No More: Ruby Payne-Scott, Who Explored Space with Radio Waves." *The New York Times.* August 29, 2018. nytimes.com/2018/08/29/obituaries/ruby-payne-scott-overlooked.html

NASA. "What Are Sunspots and Solar Flares?" *Space Place.* spaceplace.nasa.gov/solar-activity/en/

LAB 17

Atomic Heritage Foundation. "Chien-Shiung Wu." atomicheritage.org/profile/chien-shiung-wu

National Park Service. "Dr. Chien-Shiung Wu, The First Lady of Physics." nps.gov/people/dr-chien-shiung-wu-the-first-lady-of-physics.htm

LAB 18

National Geographic. "Weather." nationalgeographic.org/encyclopedia/weather

National Science Foundation. "Warren M. Washington (1936)." nsf.gov/news/special_reports/medalofscience50/washington.jsp

Warrilow, Chrissy. "Dr. Warren M. Washington: Atmospheric Researcher and Living Legend." gpb.org/blogs/talking-storm/2012/02/20/dr-warren-m-washington-atmospheric-researcher-and-living-legend

LAB 19

NASA. "Stars." imagine.gsfc.nasa.gov/science/objects/stars1.html

Specktor, Brandon. "How Stephen Hawking Transformed Humanity's View of the Universe." *LiveScience*. March 14, 2018. livescience.com/62017-stephen-hawking-legacy.html

Wikipedia contributors. "Stephen Hawking." *Wikipedia, The Free Encyclopedia*. en.wikipedia.org/w/index.php?title=Stephen_Hawking&oldid=1025849037 (accessed June 7, 2021).

LAB 20

NASA. "NASA Armstrong Fact Sheet: Sonic Booms." August 12, 2017. nasa.gov/centers/armstrong/news/FactSheets/FS-016-DFRC.html

NASA. "Christine Darden: From Human Computer to Engineer." August 26, 2019. nasa.gov/image-feature/christine-darden-from-human-computer-to-engineer

Sharlach, Molly. "Pioneering NASA engineer Darden shares her journey from 'human computer' to expert in supersonic flight." November 22, 2019. princeton.edu/news/2019/11/22/pioneering-nasa-engineer-darden-shares-her-journey-human-computer-expert-supersonic

Wikipedia contributors. "Christine Darden." *Wikipedia, The Free Encyclopedia*. wikipedia.org/w/index.php?title=Christine_Darden&oldid=1026809620 (accessed June 7, 2021).

LAB 21

BBC Beautiful Minds. "Jocelyn Bell Burnell on Truth and Understanding."

Journeys of Discovery. "Jocelyn Bell Burnell and Pulsars." youtube.com/watch?v=z_3zNw91MSY

Walsh, Louise. "Journeys of Discovery: Jocelyn Bell Burnell and Pulsars." cam.ac.uk/stories/journeysofdiscovery-pulsars

LAB 22

Lemelson-MIT. "Valerie Thomas: Illusion Transmitter." lemelson.mit.edu/resources/valerie-thomas

My Black History. "Valerie Thomas." myblackhistory.net/Valerie_Thomas.htm

NASA. "Landsat Science." landsat.gsfc.nasa.gov

NASA. "Valerie L. Thomas Retires." September 1995. nssdc.gsfc.nasa.gov/nssdc_news/sept95/04_j_green_0995.html

"Physics demonstrations: The Phantom Lightbulb." *Skulls in the Stars*. April 17, 2014. skullsinthestars.com/2014/04/17/physics-demonstrations-the-phantom-lightbulb

LAB 24

Black Women Podcast. *S2E10 Black Feminist Physics: A Conversation with Chanda Prescod-Weinstein*. open.spotify.com/episode/2yZWxC5MzrKTGwoHBQtbPF

Castelvecchi. Davide. "Dark-Energy Mapper Will Reconstruct 11 Billion Years of Cosmic History." August 12, 2019. nature.com/articles/d41586-019-02424-8

Ferreira, Becky. "The Physicist and Social Theorist Fighting for Equality in Science." *Vice*. December 4, 2020. vice.com/en/article/5dpdpd/the-physicist-and-social-theorist-fighting-for-equality-in-science

Prescod-Weinstein, Chanda. "Chanda Prescod-Weinstein: Theoretical Physicist & Feminist Theorist." cprescodweinstein.com

Prescod-Weinstein, Chanda. *Fields of Cosmological Dreams*. August 15, 2017. youtube.com/watch?v=bAqseJNNC7E

LAB 25

IF/THEN Collection. "Burçin Mutlu-Pakdil: Postdoctoral Researcher." ifthencollection.org/burcin

Mutlu-Pakdil, Burçin. "About Me." burcinmutlupakdil.net/about-me

Mutlu-Pakdil, Burçin. "TED2018: A Rare Galaxy That's Challenging Our Understanding of The Universe." ted.com/talks/burcin_mutlu_pakdil_a_rare_galaxy_that_s_challenging_our_understanding_of_the_universe?language=en

NOVA. "Who Needs Galaxies?" pbs.org/wgbh/nova/article/galaxies-faber

University of Chicago. "'Groupie' galaxies orbiting Milky Way tell us about dark matter, how galaxy formed." *Phys Org*. May 18, 2020. phys.org/news/2020-05-groupie-galaxies-orbiting-milky-dark.html

Wood, Charlie. "The New History of the Milky Way." *Quanta Magazine*. December 15, 2020. quantamagazine.org/the-new-history-of-the-milky-way-20201215

Zakeer, Fehmida. "Meet the woman who discovered a whole new type of galaxy." *National Geographic*. November 21, 2018. nationalgeographic.com/science/2018/11/meet-woman-discovered-new-type-galaxy-burcin-mutlu-pakdil-astrophysics

ACKNOWLEDGMENTS

I am extremely grateful to the team of talented people who made this book.

First, I would like to thank the team at Quarry books: acquiring editor Jonathan Simcosky, art director Heather Godin, project managers Renae Haines and Nyle Vialet, copy editor Jenna Patton, marketing managers Angela Corpus and Mel Schuit, and the entire design and editing team. I am lucky to have such a skilled, supportive group to work with.

Thank you to my brilliant, cheerful literary agent, Rhea Lyons.

Special thanks to Nadya Mason, Chanda Prescod-Weinstein, and Burçin Mutlu-Pakdil, for allowing me to include them in the book as inspiring examples of modern physicists.

Thank you to photographer Amber Procaccini for capturing the science projects and kids so beautifully. Thank you, Bridget, Claire, Divya, Elizabeth, Gladys, Grayden, Haakon, Hadley, Henry, Ivy, Jackson, Joe, Julian, Khloe, Kirin, Mark, Matilda, Raina, Ravi, Scarlett, for being amazing model scientists. Thank you Kelly Anne Dalton for bringing the scientists in these pages to life with your gorgeous illustrations.

Finally, thank you to my family and friends—especially Ken, Charlie, May, and Sarah.

ABOUT THE AUTHOR

Liz Heinecke has loved science since she was old enough to inspect her first butterfly. After working in molecular biology research for ten years and getting her master's degree, Liz left the lab to kick off a new chapter in her life as a stay-at-home mom. Soon she found herself sharing her love of science with her three kids as they grew, journaling their science adventures on her online educational platform KitchenPantryScientist.com.

Her desire to spread her enthusiasm for science to others soon led to regular TV appearances, speaking engagements, and her books: *Kitchen Science Lab for Kids* (Quarry Books), *Outdoor Science Lab for Kids* (Quarry Books), *STEAM Lab for Kids* (Quarry Books), *Star Wars Maker Lab* (DK), *Kitchen Science Lab for Kids, Edible Edition* (Quarry Books), *The Kitchen Pantry Scientist: Chemistry for Kids* (Quarry Books), *The Kitchen Pantry Scientist: Biology for Kids* (Quarry Books), and *RADIANT: The Dancer, The Scientist and a Friendship Forged in Light*, an adult nonfiction narrative about Marie Curie and Loie Fuller (Grand Central Publishing).

Most days, you'll find Liz at home in Minnesota, writing, reading, creating science experiments, singing, playing banjo, gardening, running, and feeding hungry teenagers.

Liz graduated from Luther College with a B.A. in art and received her master's degree in bacteriology from the University of Wisconsin, Madison.

ABOUT THE PHOTOGRAPHER

Amber Procaccini is a commercial and editorial photographer based in Minneapolis, Minnesota. She specializes in photographing kids, babies, food, and travel, and her passion for photography almost equals her passion for finding the perfect taco.

Amber met Liz while photographing her first book, *Kitchen Science Lab for Kids*, and she knew they'd make a great team when they bonded over cornichons, pate, and brie. When Amber isn't photographing eye-rolling tweens or making cheeseburgers look mouthwatering, she and her husband love to travel and enjoy new adventures together.

ABOUT THE ILLUSTRATOR

Kelly Anne Dalton is a professional artist and illustrator living in the Victorian gold rush town of Helena, Montana. Working from her charming 1920s studio, Kelly Anne loves creating a wide range of work, from pattern design to children's books. With a degree in economics, Kelly was happy to combine her love of historical research and science in her illustrations.

When not drawing, Kelly Anne enjoys trail running in the mountains, playing with her dogs, and traveling with her husband.

INDEX